PRESENTED TO:

_____

PRESENTED BY:

_____

DATE:

_____

PEOPLE ARE NEVER THE PROBLEM

A NEW PARADIGM FOR RELATING TO OTHERS

by
Robert Watts Jr.

Honor Books
Tulsa, Oklahoma

People Are Never The Problem:
A New Paradigm for Relating to Others
ISBN 1-56292-492-3
Copyright © 1998 Robert Watts Jr.

Published by Honor Books
P.O. Box 55388
Tulsa, Oklahoma 74155

Development Editor: Cristine Bolley @ Wings Unlimited,
2448 East 81st Street, Suite 140, Tulsa, OK 74137

DEDICATION

This book is dedicated to:

All those who have been made to feel they are a problem.

All those who have courage enough to admit they have treated others as if they were problems.

All those who have discovered the strength to stop viewing themselves as problems.

All those who wish to stop viewing others as problems.

And to my mother, Dorothy Morton,
whose love upheld me and whose words empowered me.

"The King will reply, 'I tell you the truth, whatever you did for one of the least of these brothers of mine, you did for me.'"

JESUS—MATTHEW 25:40

CONTENTS

FOREWORD
By
Ken Blanchard
Co-author
The One Minute Manager

Reading the first draft of Robert Watts' book, *People Are Never The Problem*, was thrilling for me.

I've been a Robert Watts fan since the moment I met him. He's one of the most caring, insightful and spirited human beings I have ever met. He looks at life as an ongoing learning laboratory. Nothing gets by Robert unexamined. Whenever we spend time together I go away exhilarated.

I encouraged Robert to write about the way he sees life because I felt his wisdom needed to be shared more widely. I also knew he would write something that he could share with his wife, Ellen, and their children that would be meaningful to them all. MISSION ACCOMPLISHED! The result of Robert Watts' efforts, *People Are Never The Problem*, is a gem.

If we all could internalize the simple truths in this book, the world we live in and the organizations in which we work would be better places. Why? Because we would all finally understand that "God does not make junk." People are beautiful; they're just not perfect. They have problems and they deserve our love and understanding. When we think people are problems, we corner them and give them little way out. We miss their light and focus on their darkness.

Time and time again, Robert, through his heart-warming stories, sense of humor, and self-insight, provides help for all of us to avoid this trap. You will never forget "The Medicinal Power of Mama's Words" or "Cherish the Goose Bumps" or "The Day the Doorman Saved the Day." This is all Robert Watts at his best.

Above all, remember: if we focus on the problems people have and not on people as problems, we can release incredible energy. With Robert Watts as our guide, our lives can take on new meaning. Enjoy and use his insights. Take my word for it, if you read *People Are Never The Problem*, you'll never be the same, nor will the people with whom you share your life. That's the ultimate "Win-Win." Thanks Robert!

KEN BLANCHARD, FALL 1997

INTRODUCTION

It is natural for people to have problems, but it is dehumanizing to feel that *you* are the problem, wouldn't you agree?

In 1995, Dr. Ken Blanchard (Co-author of *The One Minute Manager*)asked me to team up with him to deliver an impromptu closing address at his corporation's annual training and development client conference. I asked Ken if there was anything in particular he would like me to say. He said that I could choose my topic, but he would like my talk to address the conference theme, which was "Managing Change."

I wanted to give this audience of managers a gift of truth that would last a lifetime—a gift essential for managing change, not just in the workplace but in every area of their lives.

I walked to the middle of their half circle and paused. Then I lifted the microphone and said, "Six years ago, I learned that I had contracted cancer of the lymph system, which would require chemotherapy. While I have always believed that all people are created equal, nothing confirmed it more for me then when I entered the chemotherapy clinic.

"The room was occupied by senior citizens, middle-aged and young adults, teenagers, infants, African-Americans, European-Americans, Asian-Americans, Latin-Americans, and Native-Americans. Cancer is indeed an 'Equal Opportunity Destroyer.'

"Regardless of our ethnicity, religion, sexual orientation, education, economic status, professional titles or achievements, we all had something in common— CANCER. We were all experiencing the revelation of our vulnerable human condition, and we were all scared. And yet, we found ourselves instinctively going about the business of helping each other understand that though we all had problems, we were not the problem."

I asked the managers in the audience if they had ever felt like they were a problem. Without exception, each acknowledged that he or she had felt that way at one time or another. While I did not ask if they had ever treated others as a problem, I am sure many would have agreed that they had been guilty of this at one time or another.

I concluded my remarks by assuring them that they were not a problem and could never be one, nor could anyone else—not the people they call their bosses, nor the people they call their employees, not the people they call their competition, and as much as they may not realize it, neither are their enemies the problem. I could see by their expressions of agreement that this was a truth they badly needed to hear.

In closing, I asked them to repeat after me: "People Are Never The Problem; People Have Problems."

Within this premise of acceptance lies the greatest gift one human being can give to another. This book will provide practical ways to extend this gift of empowerment to others and to begin to see each individual as someone too unique and wonderful to ever be a problem.

ROBERT WATTS JR.

PEOPLE ARE NEVER THE PROBLEM

A New Paradigm for Relating to Others

How to Advance
From Being "the Problem"
to Having a Problem

CHAPTER 1

SO, WHO'S THE PROBLEM HERE?

"No one is a failure until he blames somebody else."
— CHARLIE "TREMENDOUS" JONES

Every success we will ever achieve involves relationships with other people. The Olympian may train alone, but she receives no trophy unless there are people who applaud the fastest, strongest, and greatest athlete. The musician spends hours in solitude to practice his art, but he receives no compensation unless there are people who want to pay to listen.

Inasmuch as people are necessary to our success, they can never be our excuse for failure. I have heard people complain about people whom they considered as problems in their lives. Some remember teachers who seemed to single them out in the classroom and humiliate them, or the bosses who wouldn't recognize their contributions, or the spouses who didn't support their dreams. It's true that when people frustrate our own ambitions we tend to see them as a problem.

What we often miss in our accusations is that they have problems of their own that keep them from participating in our ideals.

If someone has made you feel as though you are the problem in his or her life, it is vital that you remove this destructive label from your self-image. You are never the problem; you may, however, have problems that hurt the people around you. But as long as you believe that you are the problem, you will be stuck in a ditch of defeat.

Climbing out of ditches often requires help from other people, so despite the pain we may experience in the process—we must never stop loving people. It is through loving people that we are actually the kindest to ourselves. Just as people are vital to every success, they are also vital to most solutions.

I am grateful to the people who contributed to my success in life. My scholarship to a boarding school, my college career, and the opportunity to play professional football all stemmed out of relationships with people. To be successful I had to learn that people are never the problem. I had to overcome the thought that I was the problem and understand that the problems I did have could be solved.

I believed I was a problem, from the time I was a small boy; because my father had left us when I was only one year old. As a result, I concluded that I must have been a problem to him. I entered into a pattern of thinking that I had to do more, be more and prove to be the best. I believed that if I wasn't a problem, my father would have wanted to be with me.

Distracted by deep disappointment, I found it difficult to concentrate at school. My teachers soon labeled me as one of their "problem kids" and saw to it that I repeated classes. No one realized that I had a problem, they just saw me as a child who created problems for them since I wasn't learning.

WHAT HAPPENS TO A DREAM DEFERRED?

As a young teenager, I learned the difference between people *being* a problem and people *having* problems from watching the life of my stepfather, John "Johnny" H. Costen. Because of him I would later understand what Langston Hughes meant by his poetic question, "What happens to a dream deferred?" In the poem, Hughes answers the question by using an event in nature—a metaphor for describing the terrible consequences the passing of time places on an unexercised idea. Hughes compares it to a raisin in the sun: it dries up, rots, and dies.

John H. Costen had all the talent in the world and could have been whatever he wanted to be and then some. At 5'9" and weighing about 160 pounds, he possessed the finely cut features and good looks of a once removed person of African-European ancestry. He was always well groomed and manicured. He sported a thick growth of jet black hair that he wore in a high fade. His rich black mustache was full across the front of his lip and tapered off to fine points at the corners of his thin mouth. It seemed to grow broader whenever he offered his tireless smile.

Johnny had tremendous skills in mathematics, accounting, history, and politics. He combined his mastery of formal education with a strong love and physical aptitude for sports. He earned a scholarship to attend Morgan State College, but was drafted into service for the Korean War and transferred his scholarship to his younger brother who later graduated from the school.

Johnny told the story about his scholarship three or four times a year with the emotion of a martyr. He knew that in giving the scholarship away he had made the ultimate gesture any person in his generation, my

generation, or my sons' generation could make: he
had passed on the key to new worlds both physical
and spiritual. With an education you can soar like a
bird to all levels of opportunity; you can think thoughts
that only an education can ask you to think. Johnny
knew that through education you can find freedom,
and he struggled with that loss all of his life. He sadly
held on to his loss and was jerked into a decline as if
he had held onto an anchor thrown into the sea.

For years he worked at one of the largest department
stores in New York as a tailor's assistant in the dry
cleaning service—Because he was bright and good with
numbers, he was always asked to participate in the
quarterly inventory. He was the only African-American
asked to help in this way. He was never compensated
for this service monetarily with promotions or raises,
but he was given new dresses for my mother.

PROBLEMS DEFER DREAMS

This was Johnny's life after being a sergeant in the
United States Army. As time passed he began to stay
after work on Fridays to drink a few glasses of scotch
with the boys. Little by little his time with the guys
included Saturdays, then Sundays, Mondays, Tuesdays,
Wednesdays, and Thursdays, and then it would start

all over again on Friday. The good times I had experienced with Johnny and my little brother, sitting up on
Tuesday nights to watch the New York Knickerbockers,
Saturday Night fights, or Monday night Yankee games,
were gone.

As Johnny continued to drink heavily, he fell out
of favor with my mother, and they fought all the time.
We tried hiding his alcohol, but he would plead with
us kids to tell him where it was until we felt so sorry
for him that we gave in to the obvious hold that his
problem, his disease, had on him. Eventually he lost
his job and a string of jobs to follow. As Mama
became more withdrawn from him, he seemed to
drink more.

Many people who met Johnny during this stage of
his life would have said he was a problem. Alcohol
and all, I loved Johnny even though he was a tragic
figure in my life. He was the man who helped me
make my first snowball, who held me erect so I could
learn to walk, and who showed me how to box; he
was the only father I ever knew, even though I called
him "Johnny." I wanted him to be healthy. I didn't
know about things like paying rent, but I did remember about the tender times before he had a problem,
when he used to surprise me at my little league foot-

ball practices. He would ride the train home from work and come to the field across from Yankee Stadium where my team practiced. It gave me strength to see him watching through the cyclone fence as my team practiced. I felt he really loved me.

Sometimes he would stay until practice was over and we'd walk the seven blocks back to our house. He would tell me about the good and the bad in my game. When there was about a block to go, he would often snatch off his hat and with a folded newspaper in his hand he would take off running, yelling, "I bet you I can beat you home!" He always did beat me; even when I got older and threatened to win, he physically held me back so I wouldn't beat him. I'd yell at him and complain to Mother of his unfair race. But I loved his attention, and I really loved Johnny Costen.

After many months of Johnny's drinking habit, my mother had given up on their relationship, their marriage, and finally on the person. I would be forced to learn that while people are indeed never their problem, unless they can take steps to correct their problem, they will lose to it.

I could see that Johnny loved my mother and he loved all of her children, but an addiction to alcohol drove a wedge between him and the people he loved.

What started as a drink to relax him from life's tensions became a drink that helped him with the pain that comes from drinking. Eventually, he became a victim to all the illnesses associated with alcohol, including liver damage, heart attacks, memory loss, depression, anxiety, and a myriad of other problems that lead to a slow death. Getting rid of the pain became Johnny's preoccupation in life. No matter how much he loved us, his first obligation was to mask the pain.

Problems Wear Out Relationships

Johnny's problem simply wore Mama's and his relationship down to the last nerve. Johnny had been making promises to quit drinking for years, but he was too sick to get better on his own and refused to admit he needed help. To save her sanity and the welfare of her children, Mama finally put Johnny out. This time, she even packed up Johnny's clothes.

She had threatened to put him out before. He would even disappear for a week at a time but would always return to talk his way back into her soft heart. I began to think that this was the way life was for everyone—that this sick, toxic entanglement they called marriage was all quite normal. I'll never forget the cold, numb feeling that the sight of three large boxes

neatly stacked at the side of the front door gave to me.
She had never gone this far before.

Strangely enough, Johnny was sober that night
when he came home. The night he needed to be the
strongest, he had the soberness to respond. But there
was no hope left for him. Mother couldn't listen to
any more promises. The memory of that night is still
painful to reexamine.

I remember watching him through the window
curtains as he struggled to load the boxes into the
trunk of a cab. I watched him as he pulled the tails of
his coat out of the way. I caught the measure of his
eyes as he glanced back out of the corner of the
window and saw that he seemed more sad than mad.

I couldn't ever imagine Johnny getting mad. I
worried about him as days passed without any sign
of him, and as the days dissolved into weeks I slowly
turned my focus elsewhere. I knew there was nothing
I could do to help Johnny Costen. So I filled my days
with chores and activities, but in the back of my mind
I wanted to see Johnny.

The years passed painfully, as they do in impover-
ished neighborhoods. Friends died in their youth from
preventable diseases like overdoses and "friendicide"
(friends committing a suicide together). More relatives

succumbed to alcoholism, and mental illnesses were common occurrences. Somehow I managed to step over and work my way past the urban landmines that were claiming people whom I loved.

I believe that my fixation on finding something to be good at helped me to miss the party all my friends were having with drugs and girls. I was seriously looking for some way to be perfect, as if that would make the feeling of loneliness go away. I had, through my strength of character, intelligence, and sheer will, invented a self that allowed me to escape the grip of the "dream robber," the same one that deferred Johnny's dreams.

I would not be stopped by any negative element in my environment that petitioned for my soul. No gang peer pressure would sway me. No self-hate would cause me to slide into the proverbial den of the chemically dependent. No desperation to be cared for or to be a caretaker would manipulate me into being a teenage father.

SOLUTIONS MAKE THE WAY
FOR OTHERS TO SUCCEED

It was eight years before I saw Johnny again. I had secured a scholarship not only for myself but for my younger brother, Johnny's son, to a boarding school in New Hampshire. The meeting with my stepfather was a special occasion for me for selfish reasons, because it gave me an opportunity to see and hear how proud Johnny was of me for getting his son, Johnny Boy, a scholarship to boarding school.

Because I had risen to the occasion and had beaten the odds, I had put myself in a position to help my little brother. I had secured a future for Johnny's namesake, and I realized that through my own success I had done something to help Johnny Costen, after all. I was full of excitement the day I decided go with my brother to visit Johnny. I will tell you about our visit in Chapter Twelve.

The story about my stepfather is just one example of the people in my life who had problems. I was fortunate to learn that people who have problems are not an excuse for failure in my own life. I recognized that, in spite of Johnny's problems, he had a good heart and made valuable contributions to the formation of my character. Through him I learned that problems defer dreams but solutions make the way for others to succeed.

People don't keep us from succeeding—unsolved problems keep us from succeeding. On the contrary, people are our motivation to succeed. To blame others for keeping us from happiness, fulfillment and contentment is to waste creative thinking time that we could be using to solve the real obstacles to our success. While I defend the concept that people are never the problem, I also support the fact that people do have problems, and if we can help them with their problems, we also help remove the obstacles in the way of our own goals.

A friend wrote to me who heard me teach that people are never the problem and that we all need help to overcome problems in our lives. She knew I would enjoy the story of her encounter with a young man who was selling magazines in her neighborhood. A portion of her letter follows:

Dear Robert:

Your vibrant passion for people to understand that problem bearers need encouragement, not more judgment, has made an important impact on my life. Recently, a fine looking young salesman came to my house. I recognized the familiar maga-zine folio in his hand as soon as I opened the door. I didn't want magazines, but as I smiled at him and said "Hello" the words of Jesus that you quoted in your lecture passed through my mind whispering, "I

was hungry and you didn't give me anything to eat."
So I asked him what it was that I could do for him.

He seemed a little startled and asked, "May I ask
you why you weren't afraid of me? Why did you
smile when you opened your door?"

"Why would I be afraid of you?" I pretended
naiveté, knowing we teach our children never to
open the door to strangers if they are home alone.

"Because everyone else in your neighborhood
seems so full of fear. Some won't open the door;
they just shout at me through their window that
they don't want whatever it is that I am selling. One
man called me a name and said that he didn't care
what I was selling but he didn't want me coming
around to his house ever again. I'm nineteen years
old, and I've never seen anything like this back
home in Los Angeles."

I suddenly felt very sorry, and I tried to console
him by telling him that my own daughters have a
difficult time selling their fundraising gifts to
people in our neighborhood so he mustn't feel like
it had something to do with him personally.
"People just don't like solicitors approaching the
privacy of their home," I concluded.

The young salesman insisted that their reluc-
tance towards him was fear. Again he asked me why
my attitude was different. So I was honest with him,

"I can see by the look in your eyes that you are a good person; and I know God loves you, so I love you, too. It's sadly true that some people have problems with fear. In fact, the Bible says that in the last days men's hearts will fail them for fear. It isn't about you," I explained to him, "it's about a time that we are in and a problem that we must all work together to solve. But *you* are not the problem, and the man down the street *has* problems that you must ignore since he doesn't want to be helped."

Mr. Watts, I just told him what you said in your lecture about problem bearers and problem solvers. Then he told me a wonderful story about a customer he had met in Tulsa, Oklahoma, who was a problem-solver for him.

He said, "When the lady of the house told me she was going to get her husband, I thought *Oh great, here comes the part where he tells me they don't want anything and he shuts the door in my face.*

"But instead, her husband opened the door and smiled just like you did. He said to me, 'Come in, sit down, would you like some pop or water to drink?' I thanked him, and before I could tell him why I had knocked on his door he asked me, 'What do you need for me to do for you?'

No one had ever asked me that before, so I just explained that I was trying to earn a living for my son, and that I get extra credit if I can sell three magazines on one order. I showed him the list that gives me a 50% commission instead of 35% commission and pointed out the different rates for the one to five year subscriptions. That man gave me an order for two hundred dollars and that one order fed my son for a week.

Then he told me that his name was Rev. Eastman Curtis. He said that Jesus Christ cared about me and so did he. He even gave me his phone number and e-mail address so I could contact him if I ever needed him for any reason at all. That Rev. Curtis was a great salesman! I'm young, and I've studied several religions. No one in those other religions has ever given me the kind of acceptance that Eastman Curtis gave to me in the name of Jesus."

Then the young man explained that the magazine organization that he was working for finds young men and women on the streets, like himself, and trains them to sell and serve mankind in order to earn their own living. Through daily instruction, motivational videos, and morning prayer, they are shown how to serve society while earning a living.

I was suddenly aware that our conversation wasn't about magazines; it was about our interdependence on each other. I am now more sensitive to the person on the other end of the "sales pitch" since I met this young magazine salesman, because I realize that, with each individual, I am encountering a treasure that will add to the growth of my own character. I never would have had this conversation with this young man if it hadn't been for your lecture on how we should relate to other people.

Yes, I ordered three magazines, and now I look forward to new ideas on gardening, bird watching, and success for my career, all because a fine young man named Hugh took time to knock on my door.

This example of a human encounter made me think of a story from the book, *Life is Tremendous*, by Charlie "Tremendous" Jones. Charlie tells about a man who dreamed he received a million dollars and quit his job because he no longer needed the money. But the next day his water and electricity had been turned off, the paper wasn't in his driveway, and the bus didn't show up to take him into town. Soon someone came by and told him that everyone in town had received a million dollars and had quit their jobs because no one needed to work anymore!

WHAT IF NO ONE NEEDED MONEY ANYMORE?

What if you were suddenly "self-sufficient"? The truth is, our need for interdependence is great. We depend on each others' skills and talents in order to live the level of life we want to enjoy. We don't work for money; we work for people. Money is a great benefit for our service to others, but even if we didn't need the income, we would still have a basic need to exchange services with other people.

Solomon, the Jewish king, was named by God as the wealthiest and wisest man that ever lived. Solomon wrote the book of Ecclesiastes, and in Chapter 2, verse 24 (NIV), he said, **"A man can do nothing better than to eat and drink and find satisfaction in his work. This too . . . is from the hand of God, for without him, who can eat or find enjoyment?"**

SOLUTIONS SOLVE UNHAPPINESS

It isn't money that brings us satisfaction from our work, because Solomon certainly didn't need to work for the money. We work, because only through serving others do we find true satisfaction for our souls. It's a mystery that has been interwoven into our most basic source of contentment. This is why we can never see people as problems, we must see them as people with problems that we may have the skills or talents to help solve.

We especially find contentment when we are the problem solvers instead of the problem bearers. It is in our own best interest to build up one another so that we will have a strong society full of people who are eager to help others succeed in their work.

- Who are the problem bearers in your life?
- Is there a co-worker who spreads unjust complaints about you?
- Is there a teacher who is difficult to understand?
- Is there a neighbor who keeps borrowing without returning your favors?
- Is there a family member who consistently imposes on your plans?
- Is there a boss who hasn't recognized your hard work?

In spite of the obstacles that people can impose, people can never be our excuse for not achieving what we want in life. It's true that what other people expect from us can create problems for us to work through. It's true that people who have problems are often insensitive to the problems they create for others. But the people, themselves, are never the actual problem.

We can either help problem bearers solve their problems, or we can avoid problem bearers to keep their obstacles from becoming our own. What will you do? Can you be a problem solver for any of the people you listed? People can be rescued from their problems if they can be helped to understand why their actions cause problems. People can be helped when they learn how to change the actions that are causing problems.

Every success I've had in life was either the result of receiving help through a problem from someone or through giving assistance to another person who had a problem. People are not meant to walk this life alone. We are a stronger community when we work together. We are happier when we focus on solving others' problems than when we focus on ourselves.

We are fulfilled by discovering ways to change the patterns that lead to danger and disappointment. The examples I share in this book illustrate the power to break the problem bearers' cycle, whether the problems belong to you or someone else. So follow me through the journey from being the problem, to having a problem, to finding the freedom to solve the problems.

CHAPTER 2

PEOPLE ARE NOT THE PROBLEM

Problems seldom go away without the help of a problem solver.

We must not see people as one with their problems. To do so delays our ability to find a solution for their problem. Problems are situations that can be solved and even eliminated. People are not "situations" and they cannot be eliminated to resolve a problem! And even when a problem is resolved in one person's life, the same problem eventually shows up in someone else's story.

People have referred to individuals as a problem for so long that *Webster's New World Dictionary* defines problem as n. 1.) a question proposed for solution or consideration 2.) a question, matter, situation or *person* that is perplexing or difficult – adj. 1.) Presenting a problem of human conduct or social relationships 2.) very difficult to deal with; esp., very difficult to train or discipline [a problem child].

Keep in mind that the dictionary *describes* how people use words, but it doesn't *prescribe* the correctness or accuracy of the usage. For example, only a few years ago the word "prioritize" wasn't listed in the dictionary. But people constantly use the noun "priority" as a verb by saying, "Please prioritize these tasks for me," instead of saying "Please list these tasks in order of their priority for handling." Eventually the word was listed as a verb, because the dictionary describes the meaning of how words are commonly used.

But regardless of how the dictionary describes the use of the word "problem," people are still never the problem. I realize that to defy a definition in the dictionary is a bold challenge, but as this new paradigm, that people are never the problem, spreads throughout the world, we will regain the hope of seeing people apart from their difficult behavior and recognizing people as individuals in need of love and assistance.

For example, what is the difference between someone drowning in a river and someone drinking up the worth of the family's mortgage at the local pub? Let's assume that both of them were once responsible breadwinners for their families and neither person thought that his initial actions would cause a problem. Yet, both are drowning in a problem that leads to death, and they differ only in the urgency of their problem.

The drowning victim and the victim of alcohol both demonstrate behavior that is symbolic of a problem in their lives: one couldn't swim and the other couldn't stay sober. Both demonstrate problems symbolic of being unprepared for survival against the obstacles in their lives. Each person demonstrates outward signs of being in serious trouble. Both will, no doubt, die without immediate intervention.

WHO WOULD YOU HAVE A TENDENCY TO HELP?

In the above example, who would you say is the problem bearer?

Who would you say is a problem?

From what past experiences with these types of situations would you make those choices?

For now, let's consider our two problem bearers.

Neither person is *the* problem, yet we see that a problem is draining life from both of them. Dying is the problem "symbolic" in each case. They both demonstrate symptoms of the problem to show us they need help.

One problem bearer signals his problem by yelling for help while slapping the water with his flailing arms and hands. Through his body language of bulging eyes and mouth gaping for air, we clearly understand the man has a problem and needs our immediate help. In the other case, the problem is symbolized by symptoms that are more difficult to recognize at first. His signals for help include the self-destructive behavior of excessive drinking to the point of intoxication and perhaps even reckless driving. His problems are symbolized by his disregard for his appearance and an apparent lack of consideration for dependents. Other symptoms may include a damaged liver and low self-esteem.

We tend to look at the alcoholic as a problem because his behavior may be vulgar, but we may view the behavior of the drowning victim as a desperate plea for our help. Again I ask, "What is the real difference between them?" When their problems run their full courses, a clear separation occurs between the problematic symptoms and the actual problem.

Should both people unfortunately succumb to dying, their behavioral symptoms will disappear. Suddenly the water where the person was struggling will become calm, and the empty seat at the pub counter will be unnoticed. But the same problem will find another victim, because when the conditions are right the problem will reappear in someone else.

PROBLEMS ARE CONDITIONAL

A problem is dependent upon conditions. In other words, problems are often born when a noun (person, place or thing) lacks the necessary skills to resolve conflicts performed by another noun.

Perhaps the drowning person's problem began with his inability to swim. Or perhaps, the person developed a severe abdominal cramp or found the water too cold and deep. Let's heighten the conditions by proposing that this person broke the rules of canoeing and went out alone on the river and somehow got separated from his craft. Worse yet, he may have neglected to put on a life preserver. If any combination of these conditions existed, then the situation was perfect for the conception and nourishment of a problem.

The big question is: When does the problem bearer become the symptom of the problem or what I call, "the problem symbolic?" The answer is never! The two dying people we have just observed never became their problems which were "drowning" and "alcoholism." They did become victims of their problems, but they never became the problems that are now seeking someone else to victimize.

The person never becomes the problem symbolic of drowning even when a rescuer instinctively jumps into the water in an attempt to save the problem bearer from his problem. The rescuer always knows that the person he is trying to reach is not the problem; he knows that drowning is the problem, even when his adrenaline has worn off and he realizes the water is bone-chillingly cold. Even when the rescuer's muscles become rigid, when movement is difficult and his own thought processes are suddenly unclear, he does not forget that he is saving a person from a problem. Even when the rescuer pulls the drowning person towards shore, which appears farther away than before, and without warning the problem bearer panics and struggles against him causing him to also submerge, he still knows the person isn't the problem.

Instead, the rescuer and the drowning person now share the same problem. If they find a way to work together, they might both be saved. If not, the rescuer may have to release the problem bearer in order to save his or her own life.

The conditions that bring about alcoholism or chemical dependency are less obvious than drowning and more frequently misunderstood. A victim of chemical dependency may begin by using addictive substances to relieve personal, business, or social stress. The victim is more often a man than a woman and most often between the ages of thirty-five and fifty-five years of age. Problem bearers with one chemically dependent parent are fifty percent more likely to become chemically dependent themselves. Some researchers report that when both parents are chemically dependent, problem bearers are ninety-eight percent more likely to develop a dependency than those whose parents are not chemically dependent.

Many health professionals believe that this correlation between problem bearers and their chemically dependent parents has more to do with their environment than their genetics. Individuals with this kind of heritage who indulge in the use of addictive chemicals run a high risk of falling victim to the terrible problem of chemical dependency.

However, even while in the clutches of this character-eroding disease, the bearer is not the problem. Even when he or she causes embarrassment and financial loss for loved ones and business associates, the problem bearer is not the problem. Why? Like the canoeist, once the individual reaches out for help, the possibility for recovery exists.

While, the chemically dependent person's recovery will take longer, the outcome is the same—the problem bearer can be separated from the problem. And, as in the first scenario, the rescuer may have to release the problem bearer in order to ensure his or her own safety. This is true when the addiction inhibits the bearer from accepting the seriousness of his or her situation (denial). This aspect of the problem begins to interfere with the bearer's ability to provide for self, family, or business.

THE EFFECT OF PROBLEMS ARE COMMON TO ALL

Except for one or two differences, the conditions remain the same for both survivors. If the canoeist's conditions include an inability to swim, that can be corrected by taking a companion and life preservers on future canoe trips. In the same way, getting medical help and counseling can preclude future problems with alcoholism. The frigid water and a genetic predisposition to chemical dependency are conditions that can be altered only if the bearer's take precautions against their problems.

And so these problem bearers must be alert to the conditions that make them vulnerable to their problems, but they must never see themselves as the problem, because in doing so their misdirected attention adds to their problematic conditions.

Sometimes the problem claims a victim. When tragedy of this nature happens, we are wise to learn from the loss by remembering what the conditions were. Perhaps next time we will be better prepared before we walk down a similar path. Above all, it is important that we forgive ourselves for not solving the victim's problem and continue to love ourselves for being able to see past the problem to the person.

People who have problems often receive anger and more problems from the people around them. But when was the last time a tree was sued because its branches hit someone in the head? Even when the injury is severe, the injured person seldom seeks retribution from the tree. Yes, he or she wouldn't have to worry about it ever happening again if they just cut down the tree. In fact to avoid another injury from ever happening again, the individual could cut down all the trees in the forest.

But it obviously would be more productive to learn to live among the trees. Otherwise, individuals injured by trees might spend their lives cutting down trees in retribution for their pain and anger without any realistic opportunity for closure.

If the injured person would have watched the tree from a distance, he may have observed many conditions which could cause the tree's branches to break off. If he had recognized the symptoms of a possible problem with the tree, he may have avoided being hit when he passed by the tree. He may have noticed that the wind, or the weight of snow and ice on its branches, or the force of the driving rain was causing the limbs to bend unnaturally. Or perhaps the tree was shedding limbs and branches because it was dying and lacked internal nutrients to keep it strong.

In the shedding of its leaves, limbs, branches, and bark, the tree serves a significant purpose for all living things. Its life cycle helps to keep a balance between the oxygen and carbon-dioxide in the air. By observing the pattern of the tree in an effort to understand what made it suddenly drop a damaging blow, the individual will realize there is a reliable way to exist with trees without becoming angry with them.

People are sometimes like trees in that they hurt and offend people near them without realizing they are doing so. A sudden response of anger from someone

they didn't even mean to hurt does not remedy the
pain they inflicted, and it only aggravates the pain
from which they already suffer. If we can understand
and forgive the problematic conditions of inanimate
objects such as trees, how much more should we seek
to understand our fellowman with whom we share
our existence?

RETRIBUTION FOR PAIN AND ANGER

Let's examine the reaction of a foraging animal to the
same problem of a tree falling in the woods to better
understand why people should not see other people as
problems. I saw a wildlife show demonstrating how
other living things in the woods react to the sound of
a mere branch falling. On the show, an animal was
foraging in the woods when a huge branch suddenly
shed and came crashing down in the animal's direction.

Without even looking up, the animal darted away
from the falling branch and out of danger. But, as
soon as the danger passed, it returned to feed on the
tender leaves and needles still attached to the branch
and those that had been dislodged as the tree
impacted the forest floor. Clearly, this animal knew
how to live among trees. It had learned that the sound

of a falling tree indicates the presence of both danger and nourishment.

It would not have occurred to the animal to attack the tree. The tree was there to help feed the animal. Even if the branches had hit the animal, nothing would have changed with respect to the purpose of the tree. It was still there to provide food. The animal was not tempted to seek retribution, because it was able to view the situation in perspective. An animal sees the tree for what its purpose is—to serve.

Perhaps on some level the animal understands the delicate and necessary relationship it has with the tree. We can be certain, however, that the animal doesn't see the tree as a problem. It has the sense to see the falling limb as problematic and seeks to avoid it, but ultimately it sees the same branch as being vital to its own existence.

Of course, the animal acted upon reflex, but we humans who hold the power of reason and the skill of analysis should be able to see the wisdom in the action of the squirrel. Like that animal, we should not be angry at the tree or at the people who incidentally offend us along our walk through life.

Anger makes it impossible to achieve that mental adjustment. Anger paralyzes the mind's ability to be creative and make meaningful choices. Anger causes the brain to strike out and attribute something intentional and personal to people, other living things, and objects.

Blame is a condition unique to humankind. We humans seek to attribute our pain and anger to others. Often, we do this because we seek some level of satisfaction or relief. Unfortunately, we do not easily see the similarity between people with problems and the falling tree limb. We tend to see people as problematic with deliberate intentions to make life difficult for us, and we often miss seeing how the problem can work to strengthen our immediate situation or our interpersonal relationships.

Unlike the forgiving animal, we humans see the tree (or the person) and the potentially dangerous limb (their problem) as the same. Several consequences occur when we think of people as problems and refuse to forgive them:

- The problem bearer's right to be loved is deferred.
- We lose the help of the true victim in solving the real problem.
- The real problem gets worse.

When we think of people as problems, we fundamentally injure their need to be loved. We get so fixed on our pain and anguish from believing the person is the problem that we forget that the situation must be a greater nightmare for the problem bearer.

Imagine for a moment that the bearer is blind to the problem. Maybe it involves a character flaw that no one has the courage, motivation, or interpersonal skills to address. The problem bearer may have gone on for most of his or her life behaving in a way that causes others great discomfort and embarrassment. Often when people cause discomfort or embarrassment, they are labeled by those they offend. The label is never a positive one—usually they are labeled as a problem.

We must remember that problems seldom go away without the help of a problem solver. We should also understand that problems reappear wherever the conditions exist for a problem to be born. The answer to dealing with the problem lies not in eliminating or alienating the problem bearer, but in loving the person and solving the problem. After all, people have problems.

CHAPTER 3

PEOPLE HAVE
PROBLEMS

*Even people with
a natural tenac-
ity to withstand
difficulties
quickly fail when
they lose faith in
themselves.*

Every day, I rejoice over the
privilege of watching and listening to my children. From them
I have learned many things,
including how to be comfortable
with my feelings. I've noticed that my children get
goose bumps on their skin when they have a thrilling
moment such as an opportunity to forgive me or their
mother or when they are moved in their heart by some
unexpected joy. Without pretense or the need to protect
a large ego, my children allow themselves to be covered
with the goose bumps that only come when they are in
touch with their true feelings.

As I have grown older, I have had to learn to allow
myself the sudden delight that brings goose bumps. In
fact, it is absolutely essential to my emotional well-
being that I continue to experience them and that I do
so as often as possible. Recently, I've discovered that
this sensation comes involuntarily, that it is a very

natural occurrence but one that I had unconsciously suppressed somewhere in the corridor between being a child and being an adult. This was the period of time in my life when I believe I first began to lose faith in myself and think of myself as a problem.

There are two specific incidences in my life that tell a story of my experience with goose bumps. The first situation occurred when I was ten years old, the other at age forty-one which I will share later in the book.

Until I was ten, I had never said the word "Dad." I never experienced the goose bumps my children seem to feel when they sing the words "Daddy, Daddy, Daddy," through the house until I answer with a "Yes," and catch them with a big hug. The first time I said the word "Daddy" was one of the happiest and saddest days of my young life; it was the day my father decided to pay my mother and me an unexpected visit after nine years of absence.

My father had disappeared on a merchant ship when I was one year old. While he traveled the world, I learned to survive without him. I do remember getting goose bumps when my mother told me wonderful stories about how handsome he was and how he had helped her in rearing my four older siblings. I used to fantasize about his ship and how he looked all dressed up in his blue merchant seaman's uniform. But mostly I dreamed of just being with him, playing catch, going to a ball game, or simply staring at him while he read the paper or shaved.

One day, I returned from Little League football practice to find my mother seated on the sofa talking with a stranger. As I walked past them I nodded a greeting, but before I could make my way to the kitchen, mother said, "Aren't you going to say hello to your daddy?" Huge goose bumps arose on my skin. They seemed the size of plums; so large that I could feel them with my hand through the thick fabric of my football pants. I was paralyzed with excitement. My mind searched frantically for what I should do next. Until that moment, I had never called anyone "Daddy" or "Father." Finally, with the room spinning from my excitement, I blurted out, "Hi, Daddy," and the goose bumps grew in intensity. Suddenly, my extended hand was swallowed up by a hand the size of a large honey-baked ham.

For the remainder of the day and into the evening, I accompanied my mother and father on their visits to the homes of old friends and relatives who had not seen my father since the day he boarded his merchant ship. My father drove a pretty new black Cadillac and wore a sharp navy blue suit. I had never felt so proud and secure before. I stuck my chest out wherever we went. I don't remember much about that day, but I do recall very clearly that everyone admired my father.

When we returned to the house, my mother sent me inside while they finished their talk in the car. But as I was leaving, my father called out to me that he wanted me to stay home from school the next day so he could take me shopping for clothes and, more importantly, show me the ship where he worked. I was delighted. "All right, Dad!" I called out as I ran and jumped onto the porch, clearing all four steps and landing with both feet.

I could barely sleep that night because of the goose bumps. Every time I thought of the dream that had come true, my body would fill with adrenaline, and my thoughts would be consumed with the joys of the coming day and all that it would include. My mind raced as I thought of seeing the huge gray ship I had imagined all my life. I was sure I could hear the other crew members saying, "Hey Bob, this must be the fine boy you've been bragging about. He's a real chip off the old block."

Despite my sleepless night, I was up at the crack of dawn. I rushed downstairs and had my cereal, ironed my shirt and jeans, polished my shoes, and even put on clean underwear! I wanted to be ready so that when my Dad arrived, none of our day would be wasted while he waited for me.

I waited by the phone for the next few hours, and then I began to pace. By noon I started to question my mother about where he might be. She tried to assure me that he would come, and since she had never misled me before, I took some comfort in her perception. I moved my vigil to a chair near the window and watched every car pass. I watched as my friends returned to school from lunch and I watched from the steps on the front porch as they walked home past my house after school let out.

Each time the phone rang, I raced to answer it, but it was never my dad. Before long it was sunset, and I watched my friends coming back from football practice. I had bragged to many of them about my dad, and when they asked, I lied and said our plans had changed and he was coming for me in the evening. I think part of me believed it.

But the evening came and went without a visit from my Dad. I went to sleep in a puddle of tears. That night I felt more pain and bewilderment than I had ever experienced before. For the first time in my young life,

I lay in my bed and thought about my father without any goose bumps. Part of me died that night.

BROKEN DREAMS CREATE NEW PROBLEMS

I stayed home for the next few days waiting to hear from my dad, but my mother finally drew the line and insisted that I return to school. I went back to school, but I was a different child from the one that had yet to meet his father. I had entered a deep depression and suddenly, it seemed that I was living in the principal's office. I began to fight with other students and show disrespect to my teachers. Soon I lost all interest in school. In fact, nothing mattered to me. I was angry at the world, and I slipped into a self-hatred, from which it has taken me a lifetime to recover.

From that day on, I thought of myself as a problem. I was convinced that I was indeed worthless—a troublesome person whose head was too large and whose grades were too low. No wonder my father had not come back for me. As far as I could see, I had no redeeming value. It wasn't long before I began to demonstrate antisocial behavior and was expelled from school for a week. A short time later, I was moved from my fourth grade class and assigned to a kindergarten class in a misguided attempt to correct my behavior through humiliation.

And so it was that I began a life without goose bumps. They had gotten me into trouble by setting me up for pain and disappointment. I was not capable of solving my problems on my own, so I developed a natural defense (similar to what many people do who have problems). I lived in a fantasy that denied the reality that filled me with so much grief. For the rest of my childhood, I lived a life of fantasy, wishing that I were someone else. I imagined that my father was a sports hero who would one day come and rescue me. In the meantime, I could not accept compliments or gifts without wondering what people wanted from me in return. Surely they weren't giving me something because they liked me.

As a teenager and young adult, I was preoccupied with the notion that I could prove to my father that he was wrong about me. I pursued success out of a sense of anger and desperation. There were times that I would run through a field of tacklers on the football field and find myself laid out in the end zone in a state of acute anxiety. I was unable to celebrate a brilliant run, because I was so terrified that I might fail, thereby proving my father was right to reject me. On the occasions that I could minimize the anxiety, I still could not enjoy or appreciate my talents or the victories they helped bring to my teams.

Two moments in particular demonstrated to me that I had become detached from my feelings. I should have had plenty of goose bumps, but I didn't. I had overcome a tremendous academic handicap in order to win a literary award at Vermont Academy, a boarding school in Saxons River. In my senior year I graduated on the Dean's list, and, as captain, I led two teams in two different sports to undefeated seasons. As the Headmaster stood and read a prepared statement about a special award that was being given to a student who demonstrated "an influence that has been unusually wide-ranging," I felt nothing, even though I knew the award was being presented to me. There were no goose bumps. I didn't feel good or bad. Instead, I felt indifferent to the entire moment. All I wanted in that moment was for my dad to be there to recognize me and tell me that he loved me. Nothing else mattered.

The second event in which I recognized a detachment from my feelings occurred as I was finishing my career at Boston College. I concluded my collegiate experience as a Football All-American and was chosen to play in the East-West Shrine and North-South Senior Bowl All-Star games. I was also chosen as the "Defensive Player of the Year" at Boston College and first runner up for the Scanlon Award, which was given to the senior player with the highest grade point average on the team. Soon after, I was drafted in the third round by the New Orleans Saints, even though I had undergone spinal surgery in my sophomore year.

Through all of this, I felt detached and unable to enjoy any of the honored moments that would normally bring joy to a person's life. Rather than see my achievements, I could only focus on what I imagined my dad thought of me—that I was a problem and I was worthless. Believing that you are a problem takes an emotional and physical toll on your life.

YOU ARE NEVER THE PROBLEM, NO MATTER HOW MANY PROBLEMS YOU HAVE!

Shortly after I was drafted by the New Orleans Saints football team, I realized that I had been doing everything to please my father and everybody else. I was not aware of what I wanted for me, and I didn't know who I was apart from my role as an athlete. I had used sports in a futile attempt to recreate myself. After three years of back injuries and four teams later, I retired from football. I was only twenty-seven years old.

Confused and afraid, I enrolled in a master's program at San Francisco State University. After receiving an M.A. in Speech Communication Studies, I became a member of the faculty. During my time at

SFSU, I received one of its most honored performance awards. And yet, I still did not feel good about myself.

Because I was a stranger to my feelings and had no connectedness with my true spirit, I devalued even this accomplishment and attributed it to the department not being very discerning about who they selected for the award.

During this period in my life, I suffered from such a deep depression that I constantly doubted the worth of anything I did. I learned that believing you are the problem will take a toll on you emotionally and physically. I was an example of someone who had problems in spite of apparent success. Believing that I was a problem was not diminishing my success, but it was definitely stealing my joy.

PROBLEM SOLVERS REBUILD DREAMS

I couldn't love myself or enjoy my own success when I believed that I was a problem. No one identified my pain and explained to me that people cannot *be* their problems. As long as I had problems I believed that I was unworthy of special attention. It would be years before I learned that even though people have problems, they are still lovable, dignified human beings.

The person who struggles with problems needs to develop problem-solving skills. One of the greatest weapons a person has against defeating problems is a strong sense of identity through knowing what strengths he or she also bears to use against the problem. In other words, a person needs to have a confident sense of identity and self-worth to fight problems that try to attach themselves to him or her.

Often we determine who we are by how others seem to see us. We evaluate ourselves by how we are treated by those around us. This is a most unfortunate measure, since the world seems to be filled with more problem bearers than problem solvers.

A problem solver knows how to build up his neighbor with statements that show the individual is valued. Problem solvers understand the value of equipping others with tools of self-esteem. When we are all confident and strong we are able to build a better world in which to live.

When every individual is focused on his or her talents instead of shortcomings, we can anticipate great contributions to the benefits that we share on the planet.

CHAPTER 4

PEOPLE
WITH PROBLEMS
NEED HELP

People who cannot recognize the source of their problems lack the skills to solve their problems.

Ignoring the real problem and treating people as though they are problems often causes them to strike out against their accusers or seek to avoid them. In both cases, we lose the help of the victim (the problem bearer) in the task of managing or solving the real problem.

Imagine what would happen if a psychologist approached a patient as if he or she were the problem instead of the problem bearer. Immediately, the patient would erect a wall between himself and the doctor, and the doctor, who once was perceived as part of the solution, would no longer be accepted as such.

If the patient can't share his feelings, wants, and needs, then the psychologist is significantly limited in his or her ability to help the patient come to terms with the problem. The doctor and the patient are a team, and from the moment that patient enters the office both must focus their energies on the real problem.

We put two consequences into motion when we see the problem bearer as the problem:

- The problem bearer becomes defensive.
- The real problem gets nourished indirectly.

When people act defensively to being labeled a problem, they are asking, "Why don't you like me or love me?" Every one of us seeks to be befriended, as Dr. Ken Blanchard says in his book, *We Are the Beloved*.

Some strike out as a way of coping with being labeled a problem. My relationship seminars with young people from the inner cities and some of the best boarding schools in America have revealed something common to the human family. If early in our development someone tells us that we are a problem or treats us as a problem, our response is often to strike out at the world with angry retaliation. In all likelihood, we will continue to do so until someone or something helps us to realize that we are indeed the problem bearer rather than the problem.

No more fierce competitor exists than a person who seeks to protect his or her wounded self. When a problem bearer is made to feel like the problem, he or she will feel attacked and become defensive. No one should be made to feel he or she is up against the entire world.

Often, when arguments or misunderstandings occur, they are fueled by two people who have experienced being labeled the problem. And if both respond by striking out, the real problem is nourished indirectly.

Consider what happens during a forest fire. In 1991, a section of Oakland's residential hills fell victim to the most horrific firestorm in northern California's history. I reside in the Oakland hills, and my family and I were evacuated from our home. After my wife and I had moved our children a safe distance from the fire, we watched the monstrous flames color the sky orange and red as they devoured the beautiful pine and eucalyptus trees.

We could not help but wonder how the fire had spread so quickly out of control. The fire crews were fighting the fire with water hoses, and helicopters dropped buckets of water and retardants from the sky.

Later, we realized that the fire had continued to spread because the crews were no longer dealing with the problem but rather the symptom. Strong winds and hot, dry air whipped an otherwise manageable situation into a firestorm with a personality and a disposition all its own.

Mercifully, by late evening, a fog rolled in and the winds subsided. Like the wind and the air, we are often the elements that fan the flames. We must try to focus on the real problem and avoid the negative energy exchanged in defensive struggles. While locked in a battle of blaming and finding fault, people become prey to the real problem that grows out of control and eventually consumes them. We need to love the people and douse the problems.

The Mistaken Identity

In order to avoid dousing people when we are trying to help them put out the flames of their fiery problems, we must be able to clearly separate the real person from his or her problematic symbols.

I ask you: Can the symbol of the American flag *become* the United States? Can the symbol of the American eagle *become* the American People?

No matter how hard you might try, you cannot make one noun *become* the other noun. Simply put, the unique attributes of one noun identifies it from other nouns that may be used to symbolize it and no name-calling can make one object actually become another person, place, or thing.

People who have problems do not become the problem no matter how many people refer to them as the problem. A problem can bother a person, but it cannot be a person. More importantly, we know that problems are not resolved by name-calling. Problems are solved when a root cause is revealed and reversed.

SELF-RESPECT RESTORES PROBLEM BEARERS

One of the kindest ways to help people with problems is to first acknowledge what is lovable, admirable, and honorable about them. We help others by showing them the difference between who they are and what has happened to them. Many individuals cannot tell you who they are. They can tell you the problems they have, but somewhere in the chaos of their lives they have lost their sense of identity.

Do you know what your unique qualities are that contribute to society? I will share some helpful tools to explore your lovable attributes in Chapter Ten. You will learn techniques that will even help you recognize the good qualities of your neighbors. Have you taken time to discover what skills your neighbor or co-worker may have that could help you resolve your own problems? Or perhaps you have a simple answer from your bank of knowledge that would expedite the success of someone else. Through the thrill of such exchanges the truth will soon be revealed that *people are not the problem, but together they can find answers to the problem.*

We fail to get to know people because we tend to replace the real person with a label that symbolizes how we see them. But just as we are now aware that people are not problems, we must also realize they are not labels either. People are not symbols of jobs they perform or roles they play. Within every person there is a childlike spirit that desires to do the right thing and to enjoy the peace that comes from being accepted by others.

Consequently, when we express to a person that they are one and the same with their problematic symptoms, we make the mistake of integrating people with their problems. When that happens we miss the true greatness of their value to our own lives, and we damage their hope of recovery.

Author Kenneth Burke calls man the "symbol using, symbol misusing animal." For example, your pre-birth symbol was "baby" but compared to the actual you, there is very little that the symbol can do for anyone who wanted to hold and kiss you before you were born. In order to appreciate you and show you the full expression of their love, people needed the real physical, spiritual you. Without your presence, neither you nor your admirer could benefit from the warmth and sincerity that could have been conveyed by the human touch. It is easy to understand in this illustration that the symbol is not the actual person.

When was the last time you hugged the flag that represents your country? America is great and there hasn't been a time that I have attended a professional sporting event and not saluted the American flag during the singing of the Star Spangled Banner. Still, the joy and pride I feel comes not from the stars and stripes but from the closeness I feel to the diverse members in the crowd.

I salute the flag (symbol), but I love that which it represents, the people of all nations who have come here and toiled and loved so that America can be what it is today.

Symptoms are always symbolic of a greater problem. Symptoms are the signals sent to us that someone or something is in trouble. Even worse, the symptoms reveal that something or someone is being strangled by a problem.

People are not symptoms and should never be perceived as representatives of problems. All people, both young and old, have needs in common with each other. Their problems may make them look harsh and indifferent, but inside their physical house (body) lives a childlike spirit that needs reassurance and sometimes outside assistance.

PEOPLE ARE NOUNS, NOT ADJECTIVES

In the dictionary definition used earlier, we saw that the word "problem," which is most often used as a noun, was being used as an adjective to describe a child. Nouns do not serve well as adjectives. Nouns do not modify; nouns are modified, or at least we attempt to modify them. The example in the dictionary calls the child a "problem child." Maybe what the definition means to suggest is "problem behavior." That makes a big difference. If we label a child's behavior as problematic, we can take steps clinically, if need be, to modify that behavior. But what can we do to modify the child?

Do you modify the child to be more human or less human? No, the child is a human being and will stay a human being for the rest of his or her life. Even when the body grows old, the memory and feelings that make the child a human will always be there. You do not modify the person. When children are taught to believe they are the problem, they absorb great despair. They learn to expect problems as part of their hopeless existence instead of seeking creative ways out of their painful conditions.

We do well to discipline the child for bad behavior, but we still love the child, or else we risk having an adult with unresolved problems on our hands. The negative, self-fulfilling prophecy says: "If we call a child a problem often enough he or she will begin to believe it." To believe is the first step to becoming.

Unfortunately, believing a lie ignites the power to becoming a failure. So it is natural that the child who hears that he or she is a problem develops a belief that he or she is the problem! When this belief system is settled in the child's heart, the child's poor behavior becomes a symptom (symbol) that the child believes there is no better solution to his or her dilemma.

If you are in a relationship with a child who has problems, (as his or her parent, teacher, best friend, etc.), then the child's unruly behavior can become your problem too. Anytime people with whom you have a relationship are kept from realizing their goals or personal sense of contentment, their distress can be perceived as a problem for you as well. And yet, in the case of poor behavior, whether it is a child's behavior or an adult's, the behavior is symptomatic of a problem.

People with problems need to be restored to their true identity again. When we identify people with adjectives instead of nouns we can cause them a great deal of harm. Child psychologists encourage parents to describe their children with nouns that reflect their true character in order to build their self-esteem in healthy ways. When children identify themselves according to the adjectives such as "pretty" or "handsome" that describe how they look, they can become self-conscious and feel that their value is tied only to a visual acceptance.

One of the strongest examples of harm done from identifying people by adjectives instead of nouns is witnessed by the plight of the African-American. Six hundred years ago, when African-Americans were first brought to America, they arrived with a clear understanding of who they were. They knew themselves as people from particular tribes from the third largest continent in the world. Both the name of continent and the tribe were nouns that gave them an identity, and as all people in the world, they took on the dignity of the given name of their "mother-father" village or country.

They identified themselves by their national and tribal origins—Kenyan, Nigerian, Ugandan, Zulu, Swahili. Those nouns carried a history of pride, values, spirituality, morality, hope, rituals, legends, and faith. These are nouns that help make up the essence of any people. The experiences these people brought with them from their native lands established them with a sense of inheritance that contributed to their self-esteem.

When people are deprived of the memory of who they are and from where they have come, they lose a way of loving themselves and of celebrating their history. The African-Americans were treated as if they had come from nowhere. They were called "slaves," "Negroes," "darkies," etc.

Many people wonder why some African-Americans seem like a people who are lost. The answer is that when they were stripped of their noun identity and became "adjectives"; they became confused about who they were and what they should call themselves.

Over the years, African-Americans have been identified by the adjective "Black." This term was originally a derogatory label and continued to be perceived as such until African-Americans empowered themselves and took ownership of the word by enriching it with positive perspectives and images represented in songs, art, clothing, and literature. All of these were expressions of their "mother/father" symbolism from Africa.

But no matter how enriched the reference to "Blacks" became, it still was no more than an abstract idea that lacked description and placement. As proof, this reference is fast losing its role as a representation of the greatness that truly expresses the character of the African-American people. Labeling people as "Blacks" transformed from someone's idea of using an adjective to describe someone else.

No other group of people have had their nationalities so modified by an adjective, except when some Americans of European descent identify themselves as "White People" in order to distinguish themselves from the darker-skinned African-Americans.

Europeans held on to their heritage when they came to America. We all enjoy foods and holiday traditions from their imported cultures. European-Americans such as the Italian, Irish, Danish, Finish, Polish, Dutch, Swedish, Swiss, German, Russian, British, and Scottish-Americans can go to the airport and buy a ticket to their mother-father noun country, but Black Americans couldn't buy a ticket to "Black" if their lives depended on it. You simply can't book passage on a trip to nowhere. Planes, trains, and boats don't go to adjectives; they only go to nouns.

It has taken African-Americans years to collectively agree upon an adjective-free noun identity—they are Americans first and then Africans. With the noun treasure hunt behind them, African-Americans can begin the process of repairing their self-esteem. They can now study their heritage and enrich America's eclectic celebration of cultures by bringing in the colorful strength of the African history that now belongs to America. For when a people have a clear understanding of their father/mother noun, they do things that their father/mother nouns did. Human nouns love themselves, they respect other human nouns, and they understand the differences and the similarities that exist among human nouns. They know that though people have problems, they can never become the problem!

HOW TO HELP YOURSELF AND OTHERS

CHAPTER 5

THE POWER TO PURSUE POTENTIAL

When people realize they are not the problem, their desire to live life to its fullest potential is restored.

I struggled with school because of the many personal disappointments in my family life. I was slowly slipping into depression as a result of low self-esteem because nearly everyone, except Mama, treated me as though I was the problem. By the time I was in the eighth grade I had become angry, frustrated, and depressed. Yet I was driven to watch for a way out, a way to a better life, instead of falling into the pit of apathy in which my friends had compliantly lain. While I watched my best friends submit to drugs and alcohol, I resisted their options and stayed alert to any hope of change.

Though I worked hard and was a self-starter, I am grateful for people who stepped into my life and helped me pursue my greater potential. I mention many of those people in my tribute at the end of this book. Among them, I am thankful for Bill Thomas, who walked into our neighborhood park and found my friends and me, just like the people did who found the young door-to-door salesman in the first chapter. I knew he didn't live there, and I immediately wanted to find out why he was in our park. He smiled and asked if he could play basketball with us.

He told us about a free camp that we could go to that summer. I didn't know the man, but there was something about the thoughtful way he treated us that made me want to know everything about him.

Mr. Thomas treated me like a person with potential, and he never acted like I was a problem. He took time to show me new possibilities. Once I saw outside my problems I wanted to find a way to stay in that realm of freedom. After knowing him for only a short time I knew that someday I wanted to be the one who was opening new doors for other people to walk through.

Because Bill Thomas saw me as a child hungry for positive attention and not as a problem to be avoided, I was given the opportunity to meet two men who drastically changed my life forever. The first man was Jim Schoel whom I met at the Harlem Street Academy where I learned to read and write. Jim was a bit of an outdoorsman and had been one of the people who helped establish the program called Upward Bound in the sixties. He came to Harlem with the hopes of introducing inner-city kids to the adventures of hiking and camping in the Vermont Woods. I spent two months in the woods with Jim, and in that time I learned more about myself than I had before or after that experience. I learned that I could work in a team and that people found me helpful and resourceful. Most importantly, I found that I was not a problem, but I was in fact the solution to many problems that arose from the challenges presented to us in the woods. Jim Schoel was also the man who raised the money necessary for me to attend Vermont Academy. Thirty years later he reminded me why he worked so hard for my success. He said, "Robert, you were the most visionary person I had ever met in my life. You had a determination and zest for life that required my attention." To think, I had no idea that someone had such a positive perspective of me, because at that time I thought of myself as a problem.

As I mentioned earlier, Mr. Thomas had enrolled me into the urban Little League basketball camp, and during an afternoon instructional clinic I got an opportunity to meet a star with the New York Knicks, Bill Bradley. Like Jim Schoel, Bill had been blessed with the gift of knowing that people are never the problem. From the moment I saw him I sensed he was prepared to meet me where I was, no matter how dissimilar we were according to our background cultures. Bill Bradly had graduated from Princeton University, then from Oxford in England, where he had been a Rhodes Scholar in political science. Even with all those accomplishments, he still thought enough of us poor children in Harlem to come and meet us. Knowing that he had come all that way to meet me made me feel bigger than any problems I had at that time. God knows I couldn't have gone to him.

Bill talked to me; and I believe that his words were emphatically directed to me, because what he had to say rested so heavily on my heart. They were words that I had never heard before, and they were coming from a source that I held in great esteem. I heard for the first time in my life that being a professional athlete was ephemeral, and unless you prepared yourself academically you were destined to return to the same condition from which you were working to be free. His speech changed my life.

Today such encouragement towards education is cliché, but to my young ears it was like hearing the gospel for the first time. I took in every word he spoke and made it my daily affirmation. I rejoiced when Bill Bradley became a senator years later, for he was truly a man who cared for the people and who campaigned on the ticket that people are never the problem.

IT'S EASIER TO BELIEVE IN YOURSELF WHEN SOMEONE ELSE AGREES!

I had unexpectedly received a new paradigm. I saw a bigger world that I could be a part of. Suddenly my "spaced-out" friends weren't my problem. Suddenly, the teachers who said I would never make it in life weren't my problem. I had a new view of life that was full of potential and opportunities to do and be anything I wanted. I understood that problem bearers couldn't keep me from succeeding. Instead, I met problem solvers who pointed me to a better way of living. I discovered that even people who had problems couldn't keep me from prep school, professional football, a masters degree, teaching at a university, or raising a beautiful family of my own.

Once I had a vision of what life could be, there was no turning back for me. Now I want to invest my success into helping others discover that people are not the reason they can't get to where they want to go. On the contrary, people can help launch you, and the more people you rescue from the problems they bear, the greater your chance will be at achieving your own dream even sooner.

At our greatest moments of despair, we need power to overcome our problems. We need to see our possibilities. Often, people wait until they are at their lowest point in life to seek out their Creator and ask God for help. But it is in that moment of prayer that people find the power to pursue their greatest potential. Just as we all need to realize we were created to serve each other with our unique gifts and talents, we must also discover that we are to be totally dependent upon God.

There is Power to Pursue the Greater Happiness

I have never regretted turning my life over to God. I share this personal part of my story because it was here that I found the power to pursue the greatness of life that I now know and enjoy.

After many years of lecturing and talking to others, I have discovered that my inward focus on failure was not uncommon, nor were my powerless attempts to overcome my sense of futility on my own.

I needed help in loving myself. I learned to speak up, step forward, and admit my need by first admitting that I needed God. Only when we learn to love ourselves enough to share ourselves with others do we begin to see our own potential for happiness.

I began to draw strength from prayer, and in those moments God comforted me and settled my thoughts. I recalled the times I saw God reaching out to me when I was a child. I recalled the times I had seen my Mama pray for strength to raise her children.

I recalled how He sent Bill Thomas to my neighborhood park to show me a life beyond the few city streets that I had known. I recalled the miracle that took me from the Bronx to the boarding school that I had dreamed of going to as a child, of how a wealthy benefactor, who saw my eagerness to succeed, decided to finance my tuition to the prep school. I clearly saw for the first time what a loving Father God had been to me, even when I wasn't aware of His presence. God made Himself evident to me through all His workings in my life.

I recalled my days as a prep school student at Vermont Academy and how I loved to walk among the beautiful oak, pine, and cedar trees that grew on that campus in the rich, lush soil that nourished them. I saw that my heart had to become soft like that soil so that I could receive the seed of truth that God had been sowing into my heart. I realized that God had never seen me as a problem. On the contrary, He had been moving in my life all along the way to prove His love for me.

Opening my heart to God's power was the most important decision I have ever made and is the most important decision every individual must face.

Life Needs Good Soil in Which to Grow

We need a soft heart to receive power to achieve our greatest potential. I am always moved by the reality that only soil in its softest state can feed a huge oak or pine tree. I liken the rich fertile soil to the hearts of some of the people in whom I have placed my emotional roots. No matter how I acted in the past, because of their soft hearts, they sensed I was not the problem that was directing my behavior.

It was during these moments of reflection and prayer, as I thirsted for the truth, that I came to understand that my heart had been hardened. I had believed the lie that I was the problem for so long, that my heart had become dry and parched—unable to receive the good seeds that had been cast my way many times.

If softening were to occur, I had to adjust my perspective of myself and life in general. I had to see my life from God's viewpoint, not through the eyes of a disappointed ten-year-old boy. By simply asking for God's help, I had the power to begin again.

Jesus taught that unless a man is born again, he cannot see the kingdom of God. To find my greater potential, I asked God for a chance to start over and see the plans that He had for me instead of the problems that continued to steal my sense of peace. Now, when I sometimes feel tempted to revisit my old (dis)comfort zone of self-doubt, I take refuge in prayer and find the power to hold on to life's potential instead of its problems.

During these moments of retrospection I repeat a self-authored affirmation to keep the urge for rigidity at bay: "It is when the soil is soft that it is at its strongest."

During my journey from being the problem to having a problem, I realized just how much we are like the soil in the biblical story of the sower from the book of Matthew, chapter 13. Sometimes we are hard and unreceptive to good words that could sprout up into success just like the sower's seeds. When our hearts are hardened, these seeds may bounce up and settle on the surface or lodge in the cracks.

Some seeds may dehydrate and dry up from the heat of the sun and many more may be blown away by the wind. Still others are eaten by the birds or washed away by a sudden summer shower. None of these seeds ever realize their potential. Likewise, when our hearts are hardened and impenetrable, we lock out the world.

When we are in this state, the expressed concerns and needs of those around us fall on deaf ears. Sometimes those people whose needs we ignore are our mothers and fathers, sisters and brothers, husbands and wives. Sometimes they are our children, our best friends, or our neighbors. They could even be co-workers or lost, hungry, and homeless strangers.

What causes people to become hard like the type of soil that cannot grow food to feed the hungry? I know that one reason is the accumulated hurt that results from being treated like a problem. Just as farm soil depends on the farmer to provide it with sustenance (fertilizer, water, and protection) in order to produce foods that sustain human life, so do we need the care and love of others to keep us watered with truth and fertile with a sense of self-worth so that we can help ourselves as well as others.

When the soil is soft, tender and fertile, heavy and full, we can feel its refreshment slip between our toes as we walk across it with bare feet. When it's moist and rich enough to be formed into clumps, we can scoop it up in our hands. It is then that the soil is strongest and most powerful—it can feed the entire planet and everything that lives on it. In other words, the soil is at its best when it is giving, and it can only give in abundance when it is soft. For when it is soft, it is able to receive the seed—the seed that realizes its potential and nourishes others.

THE PROBLEM BEARERS MUST BE RESTORED TO REACH THEIR POTENTIAL

Not too long ago I visited the office of one of my management consulting clients in northern California. When I entered the building, I noticed carpenters and computer technicians working all over the place. The walls had received a fresh coat of paint, and new furniture sat in boxes everywhere. New lighting fixtures and computer networking cables dotted the workplace and provided a progressive atmosphere of healthy pride.

What stood out most about the place, however, was the way the employees had learned to coexist with the construction workers without jeopardizing their productivity. I was very impressed with how efficiently the company maintained its output in the face of such an intrusion into the corporate environment. When I asked the office manager how she managed such a feat, she replied, "I gave everyone in the office an opportunity to help plan the office's makeover, from picking the construction contractors to deciding what color the toilet seats would be. They all had an opportunity to take some ownership in the process."

That was a sound approach to creating a cooperative atmosphere, but I was most impressed with something she said as she escorted me to the door, ". . . we had considered gutting the whole place, right down to the joists, but too many people fought to hold onto the basic character of the office. It was agreed that with the addition of a few elements and an update of the communication and computer systems, the office would be improved but not lost."

I thought how appropriate that office situation was as an analogy for restoring problem bearers. I imagined what the consequences would have been to the productivity of that company if they had elected to gut their workspace. By doing so, people would have had to come off line to relocate temporarily, and clients would have been negatively affected by a stoppage in service to them. The whole ordeal would have been repeated when the time came to re-enter the remodeled offices.

Simply put, this situation spelled out the principle that things do not always need to be torn down to be made better. Too often we think change means to make everything new. More can be realized from a new approach suggesting that change should be looked upon as making people and things better! When we think of changing something or someone, we too often look for what we can subtract. But a new approach may mean to add to or simply redefine.

Every semester for the past fourteen years, I've asked college students who take my speech communication course to list ten verbs that they feel represent why they love themselves and ten things they want to improve about themselves. Without fail, their minds reconfigure my question to be, "What do you want to change about who you are?"

CHANGE DOESN'T ALWAYS MEAN TO TAKE AWAY SOMETHING

When we talk about changing ourselves, we inevitably end up contemplating subtracting something from ourselves. Just as in remodeling an office, restoring the problem bearer involves, to a greater degree, recognizing what is to be added and what needs to be left alone so that it can be reconnected, loved, and admired. Unlike the office, we cannot tear people down to their joists or relocate them from their spirit while we work on their egos. We would do well to see the spirit of the problem bearer as the character of the office that was too appealing to lose and the ego as the walls that needed to be painted rather than demolished.

When we take our "people are the problem" ax to problem bearers, we end up cutting down their self-images and diminishing their zeal for life. Our words of anger and hate leave little intact. As a result, these people require a great deal to build them back up. So far down do we cut them sometimes that when they are rebuilt, they are often reinvented, and that which we loved initially—the uniqueness of their person—is lost along with the portion of our humanity that was connected to their spirit.

It makes perfect sense that those office workers opted for remodeling over reconstruction. There was a part of themselves in the place as they knew it, and they were astute enough to recognize it. Maybe by tearing the office down, they somehow felt that a part of themselves would be lost with it. If a place can cause us to feel a certain connectedness, imagine how much more a person can cause us to feel a sense of belonging if we allow our relationships to grow.

By restoring the problem bearers, we are ensuring that they can stay whole and that we will continue to be connected to them, for "loving the people" requires us to love the bearers of problems. By helping problem-bearers to reconnect with their lovable spirits, we help them to rediscover their own potential, and we subsequently contribute to their restoration as well as our own.

CHAPTER 6

THE POWER OF MAMA'S MEDICINAL WORDS

Sticks and stones will break your bones, but words can help to heal you.

We live in a world where too many people see others as problems and problems as something to hate. People are fortunate if they have someone in their lives blessing them with the soothing power of affirming words; words which will assist them in their journey through this life. Negative, accusing words sometimes hurt us, but reassuring, hopeful words possess the dual capacity to mend and restore us. It is the latter that comfort us.

What are the medicinal powers of words? Words can act as an agent for healing both the mind and the body. It is a fact that patients show faster and more reliable responses to treatment when seen by a doctor with a good bedside manner. Good bedside manner involves using words and gestures that both soothe and empower patients. Soothing words help people who are too sick to address their fear, lift off doubt, accept their fate, return to their dreams, see the bright side of things, and reconnect with hope. Empowering words help patients feel like valued resources, part of the team, and separate beings from their problems.

I am sure you can recall a few occasions when you lay in bed as a child, congested and coughing, running a slight fever. No doubt you felt terrible, maybe even afraid, but your mother's or father's words calmed you.

You probably cannot now name the cough syrup or home remedy they used. However, most likely you can remember how they introduced you to the medicinal power of healing words.

I recall some of the words my mother used to speak to me and my five siblings at times when we felt ill, rejected, defeated, or guilty. In rearing my own children, I find myself repeating a lot of these phrases and noticing the true medicinal affect they have in soothing the symptoms of many troublesome emotional and physical conditions.

Words That Comfort Us When We Feel Ill

"Mama's here!"

"Everything's going to be all right."

"Mama's going to get something for that nasty old cough."

"Mama's not going to let anything happen to you."

WORDS TO EMPOWER US WHEN WE FEEL DEFEATED

"Just remember God will always love you."

"Don't worry, together we can make it."

"Don't worry, just tell mama what's wrong."

"Sometimes life is a struggle. That's why God made you so strong."

"God won't give you something that you can't handle."

"Be proud of yourself—you tried your best."

"It's not the number of friends that counts—it's the quality."

"Take your mind off what you've lost and give thanks for what you have."

WORDS THAT RESCUE US WHEN WE FEEL GUILTY

"Whenever you need to talk, just call Mama. I'll always have time to listen."

"God's always ready to listen."

"Mama forgives you."

"God has already forgiven you."

"Mama will never give up on you."

"God knows that you are not perfect."

"Try not to be so hard on yourself."

"Lets start by saying you're sorry."

"Did you think to ask to be forgiven?"

"You can't live in the past. Forgive yourself and move on."

"You have a beautiful spirit. Don't weigh it down by feeling sorry for yourself."

As adults, my siblings and I still depend on the sound of my mother's voice and the words she uses to soothe us when we are troubled. My mother never forced us to accept her love. Her support was always unconditional. It was always offered in the form of a question or presented as a fact that we could depend on and trust. That's why it is so easy to come to her now. We know we will not be judged or criticized for having problems or for not being perfect.

Sometimes she delivered her words in an authoritative voice in order to motivate us: "You need to forgive yourself and get on with your life." But most often she left it up to us to accept or ignore her soothing and empowering words of love. As a result, we were able to incorporate much of what she said into our own communication styles. We have learned that much of what she says carries an impact no matter how it is delivered. And my mother realizes that when she has a problem, she can count on her children to give back to her the same kind of medicinal word power that she gave us in abundance.

WHO NEEDS MEDICINAL WORDS FROM YOU?

When we consider that most people spend more time with the people they work with than the people they live with, we realize how important it is to love the people in our working world. Would it surprise you to know that the medicinal power of Mama's words can also work wonders in the workplace?

I can't help but wonder what the workplace would be like if managers regularly used some of the medicinally powerful words that their mothers or some other caring person used to soothe and heal the broken places in their lives.

All of us have benefited at one time or another from medicinally powerful words. How is it then that business leaders have not learned to incorporate into the workplace what has worked so effectively at home? For example, suppose senior management directed every manager and front-line employee to come up with ten medicinally powerful phrases that someone used to soothe the pain they felt during a difficult period in their lives.

After brainstorming for a weekend, managers would be encouraged to come back to the table with their medicinal words. A company-wide task would then be to come up with two or three phrases that could be used to create a "Live It Statement"—a proactive "let's walk our talk" directive. "Live It" is a present tense command that means *now*—in this moment. A "Live It Statement" would provide management and employees with words and phrases that they could use to send the message, "I value you separately from what you do for this company." The nature of medicinal words and phrases is that they lead to immediate action and always inspire the sender and receiver of the message to be loyal to the values represented by the words or phrases.

I attended a business conference where a "Live It Statement" would have made a difference in their workplace. The guest speaker was the CEO of a major American utility company. His talk focused on the successful job his executive management team had done in downsizing the staff and repositioning the remaining employees. He talked with great pride about how the company had saved millions of dollars and in turn used some of the surplus to improve service to customers and increase marketing. These actions enabled him to report record gains to the board of directors and shareholders.

When he concluded his presentation, he opened the floor to questions, and I asked what he and his executive team had done to aid those employees who had lost their jobs in the downsizing. He hesitated for a few seconds and said, "That is a good question." Then he paused a moment longer, and said, "What would you suggest in this situation?"

I proposed a program that would use some of the surplus money to hire an outside agency or create one within the organization to help the displaced workers find jobs. This would involve identifying vocational training programs, preparing resumes, and in general, helping to lessen the emotional trauma people feel when they are cut off from an extended family—one, in some cases, they had been loyal to for many years.

I went a step further to suggest that the remaining employees must be accountable as well. Too often, after having been laid off, people are forgotten by those who remain. It's as if they don't exist anymore. Yet they had given these same associates baby showers, sent flowers of sympathy when loved ones passed away, attended weddings, and taken company vacations with them. No wonder so many people die after they are forced to retire or commit suicide after they are fired. The relationships they thought were so solid turned out to be superficial. The bottom dropped out from beneath them.

The whole room became silent as I spoke. The CEO was on the spot before an audience of top management trainers, but to his credit, he responded honestly. "I am afraid that I hadn't considered any of those options. It is something I'll have to discuss immediately with senior management. Thank you very much for your suggestions."

His response was a positive one, and it signaled hope that his company would become the kind of place where medicinal words are allowed to take some of the sting out of the harsh realities of business. Later I wondered what affect a "Live It Statement" would have had on the life of this company.

PEOPLE PERISH WITHOUT A VISION

What if the CEO had used a "Live It Statement" that said, "Loyalty is a responsibility we all acknowledge. In coming and in going, we are together." This statement suggests that while the company expects loyalty from its employees, it also recognizes that loyalty must be reciprocated, and that because we stick together, we will do whatever we can to look after one another, not only while we are employed by the company but even when we have been disengaged.

This "Live It Statement" makes the announcement that the people are the company. The next time you get a chance, drive by the building where you work after everyone has gone home for the evening. Check to see if the building does anything when the people are gone. Do the computers program themselves? Do the bathrooms clean themselves or the coffee machines put the coffee grounds and filter in place all by themselves? When the people go home, the company goes with them.

When people are laid off as a result of corporate downsizing, they often feel like they must have been viewed as a problem. However, if corporate executives used medicinally powerful "Live It Statements," they would send a different signal to the people that they have to let go. They could reinforce the principle that people are never the problem. This reassuring foundation offers a sense of self-respect to the people who must market themselves for a new position elsewhere.

We all understand that the realities of business some-times necessitate layoffs, but they need not be conducted with disregard for the employees and the part they have played in making the company what it has become.

When management says that they love their companies, I wonder if they really know what they are saying. Do they mean that they love what their companies do? Or do they mean they appreciate their employees? Because these are very different things.

If they embrace the first definition, then they will treat their employees as expendable. If, on the other hand, they understand that the company consists of the people who work there, they have made a great and profitable discovery. These are the managers who will find ways to fill the workplace with medicinally powerful words.

Mama taught us to treat each other with respect. If my mother had been a business manager, she might well have used this medicinally powerful "Live It Statement":

"People are never what they do. When we treat them as guests, what they do gets done much better."

Aren't you more motivated to work hard for someone who respects and believes in you than for someone who never has a good word for you? If you believe this, then "Live It!"

CHAPTER 7

THE POWER OF LOVING YOURSELF AND OTHERS

Self-acceptance is the first step in learning to accept others.

True love is unconditional. No one is good enough to deserve someone else's love; therefore, love cannot be earned. We all feel the greatest value when we are loved in spite of our shortcomings. There are times, however, when the only person around to love us during our moments of defeat is ourselves. Be kind to yourself, quick to forgive, and ready to try again or try something else. But at all times, avoid the destructive trap of believing that your problems are a reflection of who you are.

To enjoy our greatest purpose for existence, we must learn to love ourselves unconditionally. Then we will understand how to demonstrate unconditional love toward others.

If you see someone who is not able to love himself, then be the one who lifts him up with medicinal words of encouragement. When was the last time someone said that your actions toward them were like a sweet perfume? Have you ever met someone about whom you could say, "She was like a breath of fresh air"? As we learn to be problem solvers by being kind to one another, quick to forgive and ready to help others, we will enjoy goodness, a clear conscience, and the blessings that come from believing the truth.

The lack of vision and possibilities causes desperate symptoms in anyone who is a problem bearer. But negative actions do not always reflect the condition of a person's heart. Someone may act out of ignorance or despair, but at the core of who they are is a human being in need of a sense of self-worth in order to survive.

SUCCESS HAPPENS WHILE HELPING OTHERS

The inspiring motivational speaker Zig Ziglar has taught thousands of now successful people that "you can get everything in life you want if you help other people get what they want." To truly help people get what they want you must demonstrate your acceptance of who they are in order to win their trust to let you help them.

If love were not unconditional, the very act of childbirth would prevent most mothers from loving their children. On many occasions I've heard my wife "fuss" at our children while she was carrying them. One of our sons actually kicked her so hard during her pregnancy that he cracked her rib, and it took twenty-two hours of labor to bring another son into the world. Yet the moment the doctor placed them in her arms, she gently cooed, "Oh, my baby, it's okay. Mama's here. Mama loves you with all her heart."

However, life's reality is that love is often tested. We as human beings often are unable to recognize, manage, or avoid conditions that give birth to problems. When we see people as problem bearers rather than problems, we provide for ourselves an opportunity to nourish our love for one another. I see this as life's fitness program for developing our love muscles.

Our love muscles become stronger, more flexible, and better developed as we stretch to get past our preconceived notions about people as problems and see people as a part of the lovable solution. Of course, the opposite is also true. The more we insist that people are problems, the more atrophied our love muscles become.

I would like you to think of forgiveness as a health club for loving. The most important thing to remember about this health club is that no one needs to be asked to become a member. You are born a member of the forgiveness club. But you must use the facility in order to stay fit! You can't just wear the pin that says, "I'm a forgiver." You have to flex your love muscles and do something to reaffirm the one who has offended you. Everyone needs to be loved.

LOVE IS THE POWER TO RESTORE OTHERS

I am reminded of lines from the Lorraine Hansberry play, *A Raisin In The Sun*[1]. They help to underscore this idea of forgiveness and unconditional love in the lives of an African-American family of meager financial means. The family is living in a small two-bedroom apartment on the south side of Chicago in the early '60s.

The characters include a middle-aged widow named Leana Younger (Mama), her teenage daughter who dreams of becoming a medical doctor (Beneatha Younger), her adult married son Walter Lee Younger (Brother), his wife who is pregnant (Ruth Younger), and their son (Travis Younger).

---

[1] From *A Raisin in the Sun* by Lorraine Hansberry, pg 129. Copyright © 1958 by Robert Nemiroff, as an unpublished work. Copyright © 1959,1966, 1984 by Robert Nemiroff. Reprinted by permission of Random House and the Estate of Robert Nemiroff. All rights reserved.

The central focus of the play involves the family's anticipation of a lump sum pension payment to Mama from her husband's job. Papa has died on the job from a heart attack, and his $10,000 pension is enough to buy a house in a nice neighborhood and provide for Beneatha's college education. But Brother, in an ill-fated attempt to prove himself a man equal to the measure of his father, takes the money and invests it with two con men who predictably skip town.

An enraged Beneatha likens Brother to a toothless vermin, claiming that he is not a man. Mama grieves that death has come to her home and asks Beneatha if she is mourning for her brother. Beneatha continues to hurt Mama by disowning Brother.

Mama asks Beneatha who gave her the privilege of writing her brother's epitaph. She reminds her daughter that she has taught her to love her brother. Beneatha is startled by her mother's request. At this point Beneatha responds,

BENEATHA: Love him? There is nothing left to love.

MAMA: There is *always* something left to love. And if you ain't learned that, you ain't learned nothing. *(Looking at her)* Have you cried for that boy today? I don't mean for yourself and for the family 'cause we lost the money. I mean for

him: what he been through and what
it done to him. Child, when do you
think is the time to love somebody the
most? When they done good and
made things easy for everybody? Well
then, you ain't through learning—
because that ain't the time at all. It's
when he's at his lowest and can't
believe in hisself 'cause the world done
whipped him so! When you starts
measuring somebody, measure him
right, child, measure him right. Make
sure you done taken into account what
hills and valleys he come through
before he got wherever he is.

Those last words from Mama are profound. In the
play, Brother manages to redeem himself, no doubt
because his mother forgave him and allowed him to
remain the leader of the family despite his mistake.
He recovers and goes on to move his family into the
house that they wanted and designs a way to pool
money to secure his sister's tuition for college.

THE PURE IN HEART HEAL MORE QUICKLY

In the real world, restoring people and relationships
takes some time. Whether asking for forgiveness or

giving forgiveness, both parties must be pure of heart. A pure heart is a heart free of anger, hatred, guilt, regret, bitterness, spitefulness, disgust, reservations, sympathy, pity, charity, guile, and envy. No matter how good an actor one might be, the problem cannot be fooled.

An insincere heart is like an infection that lingers in the body because the patient did not follow doctor's orders and take the entire prescription of antibiotics. By taking less than was prescribed, the patient leaves enough of the germs in place to restore the infection, even adding to its potency. Strengthened, the infection can actually rage throughout the body until no amount of medication can save the patient.

Likewise, relationships are sometimes lost when hearts are not sincere. This happens when the one who offers forgiveness has never stopped seeing the other person as the problem. The problem then nourishes itself on the insincere heart, and the seed of bitterness that remains germinates in the heart of the one who was offended and causes his behavior and language to betray him. The old negative ways of treating the problem bearer will resurface, often with more vigor, driving the person with the problem away, maybe deeper into a belief that he or she is indeed a problem.

When both parties have sincere hearts, they work in an atmosphere of mutual respect and cooperation. When the heart is pure, it is like the earth cleared, turned, and ready for new seed. From this rich foundation comes a new crop nourished by respect and trust—values that ensure that problems remain problems and people remain people.

PEOPLE ARE NEVER THE PROBLEM;
PEOPLE ARE OUR KEEPERS.

Albert Einstein has been quoted to have said, "For what reason are we put on this earth, I am not sure, but I do know that we are here for each other."

Relationships with other people are vital both to our personal growth and our fulfillment as a society. Once people realize that other individuals are not the problem, they will be able to love and communicate with others with greater ease and sincerity.

WHEN YOU FORGIVE SOMEONE,
YOU RELEASE THE POWER TO LOVE THEM

It is impossible to love people when you see them as problems, because you deny what makes them lovable—their feelings. Feelings are those emotional responses that keep us in touch with ourselves and the world around us. Feelings help us laugh, cry, rejoice, experience humility, have empathy, accept gifts, extend forgiveness, and relate to others.

When a catastrophe hits a community, it becomes clear that people are not the problem but part of the solution. I remember when the 1989 earthquake devastated the San Francisco Bay area. A freeway collapsed during rush hour, pinning motorists in their cars. Many of the homeless who panhandled on the streets below helped fire fighters, paramedics, and the police in the rescue efforts. These people had been viewed as problems by Bay Area residents until the earth moved under their feet and the real problem was suddenly evident.

As concrete and steel fell in every direction, these down-and-out citizens became part of the solution. The poor and homeless, even the drug addicts—those who lived under the freeways and in the doorways of buildings—were the first voices that earthquake victims heard.

Those who were rescued and comforted by their voices surely did not consider them problems but blessed solutions to the problem.

We are all born with spiritual instincts, and people who want to be problem solvers need to trust these instincts. I am referring to those feelings that compel people to risk their lives for total strangers in emergency situations. Those instincts are not limited to the involuntary impulse to respond to another human being in need but also include the compassion and identification we have with all living things.

While our intelligence may separate us from other creatures, our spiritual instincts remind us of our unspoken relationship with all living things. It is our spiritual instincts that help us get past the idea that people are problems. When we experience goose bumps, our spiritual instincts are letting us know that we are connecting with other people. Something wisely pure and primal is triggered on those occasions.

Though these loving feelings are often suppressed for one reason or another, they are loosed when we allow ourselves to become involved in the act of forgiveness. In the next chapter we will explore how the act of forgiveness empowers us to love ourselves and others unconditionally.

Chapter 8

The Power of Forgiving Offenses

No one will get through this life without the need to be forgiven or the opportunity to forgive.

The need for forgiveness is a reality that exists among all living things. Forgiveness helps relationships flourish and enables the earth to replenish itself after its creatures have made a mess of things. For example, when a herd of elephants decimate a dense segment of jungle, leaving nothing—no roots, no bark, no trunks—or when lightening strikes a dry forest causing a firestorm to destroy thousands of acres and hundreds of animals, nature is quick to forgive and often gives back more than was destroyed.

Shortly after I completed my treatments for cancer, I received a letter in the mail. I immediately looked in the left-hand corner to identify the sender and was confused when I saw that the letter had been sent by someone residing in Brooklyn by the name of Robert Watts. My first thought was that friends were playing a little joke on me. I had forgotten that three years earlier

I had paid the Salvation Army to search for my natural father whom I had not seen since I was ten years old. I had long before given up hope on the whole thing.

I opened the letter and read the first words: "Dearest Son." For a moment my mind froze, and I couldn't feel my body. I do remember calling out to my wife and asking her to read the letter to me.

In the letter, my father talked about living overseas and told me that he had fathered two daughters in Germany. He was now retired and living in New York. He said that he had been looking for me for years but was unable to find me, because my mother had moved to California in the early '70s. As I listened, I felt a sense of closure. Even later that night when I called him at the number he provided in the letter and during my subsequent visit to see him the next week, I felt no goose bumps or any great sense of joy or exhilaration. Though I had made great progress in other areas of my life, I had not yet dealt with my feelings for my father.

I did a lot of soul-searching through prayer for an understanding of my lack of emotion. Part of me wanted to hate him, and the other part of me was afraid to trust him. I knew that it was time to call my mother.

When I informed my mother that I had found my father, her first reaction was in keeping with her beautiful forgiving spirit. "Thank God!" she shouted.

"Mama, I'm afraid to see my father," I responded.

She replied, in her softest voice, "Why is that, baby?"

"Because I am not sure how he really feels about me. Whether he will love me the way a man should love his son, the way I love my children—with all my heart and soul."

Then my mother said something very profound and her words held that wonderful medicinal quality I had grown to love and respect.

"Try not to hold your father to your standard of what you have become as a man. It wouldn't be fair to him or you. He will never be able to live up to that."

"Why can't he," I asked, "and why shouldn't he meet his responsibilities to me? Why couldn't he love me the way I loved my own children, especially if that was what I needed from him?"

She responded as supportively as she could, as her voice broke with sadness, "Because you had me as your mother."

And that was all she had to say. She had always showered me with love and never allowed me to wallow in hatred for my father. Sure, she allowed me to vent about what I wanted and needed. With my strong personality, she could do little else. But she always came to me when my tantrums were over and reminded me that I was a blessed child because God had seen fit to give me to a mother who loved me and worked hard to provide for me.

Recently I asked my father about his childhood. He shared with me that he was the youngest of thirteen children. He left home when he was fourteen years of age and at sixteen, became a cook's assistant on a merchant ship.

He told me that forty-six years passed before he made contact with his family again, and that in the interim, both his parents and all but three of his siblings had passed away. He also told me that he had not seen his daughters in Germany since they were three and five years of age.

TRUTH ALWAYS SETS YOU FREE

I then knew with certainty that I was not the reason for my father's lack of commitment to me. He had been leaving people behind him all his life. I also understood the courage it had required on my mother's part not to fill my head with negative ideas about my dad. Maybe she always understood that my father was a victim of something he was unable to talk about—something that caused him to be incapable of connecting with people. Perhaps he had been told too often that he was a problem.

It has now been several years since I found my dad. Every month or so we call each other and catch up on our lives. I have even met one of my German sisters and talk occasionally with the other one on the phone.

No doubt it is because of my mother's influence and her medicinal words that I am now able to love my father and resist the temptation to see him as a problem.

Too often when I speak to people who have had a similar experience with one of their parents, they express their hatred and disgust for that person. I can now tell them that if they continue to hate, those thoughts and feelings will eventually take a serious toll on their physical and psychological health. It is much better to love than to hate and to forgive than to hold onto anger.

You Should Never Hate— Not Even The Problem

The opposite of love is hate. *Hate* is defined as the intense dislike of something. The operative word here is *intense*, which comes from the middle English word *"intend,"* meaning to stretch out for or aim at. The word *"tension"* is also derived from the same root form. Tension occurs when energy is either applied as pressure to an object or person (compression or oppression) or used to pull something or someone in a direction contrary to their nature or desire.

What happens to an object when too much pressure is applied or a moderate amount of pressure is applied for too great a period of time? It will react in one or a combination of ways: increase in temperature, bend, warp, crack, or break. What is true of objects is also true of people. I am not referring to placing some heavy physical object on the human body. While this would no doubt cause the afore mentioned effects, people seldom allow themselves to be placed under such constraints.

Instead, the issue is the willful participation in creating internally the negative and harmful language and ideas that produce stress in our emotional and physical selves.

ALWAYS STRIVE TO ATTRACT THE OPPOSITE OF HATE.

Think of the tension we subject ourselves to when we allow ourselves to hate someone or something. Our bodies and minds are not designed to accommodate hatred. Evidence of this exists in the way our bodies are affected when we are in this state. Have you ever experienced the following during a state of anger?

- your face flushed with hot blood,
- your shirt collar seemingly shrinking around your neck,
- your teeth gnashing together until your jaw aches,
- your eyes bulging out of their sockets,
- your chest expanding, then tightening,
- the veins in your neck protruding,
- and your temples pulsing violently?

We experience these symptoms because our heart muscles are pumping out massive quantities of blood at a rate that the rest of the body struggles to accommodate. While our system of arteries and veins do a pretty good job managing this Herculean feat on an occasional basis, this pressure becomes too much for our bodies to handle if it continues over time. Our health will eventually suffer if hatred and anger continue to flow through us.

EGO'S HINDER SUCCESS

Our minds have generated what I call "Fear-Thought-Energy." This comes from our EGO—what Ken

Blanchard calls "Edging God Out"—and not from our "spiritual instincts."

Fear-Thought-Energy is produced when we feel we are unable to do something about a problem. When we believe we have no means to manage a situation, we sometimes become aggressive toward it. Or we may find ourselves becoming fearful of certain situations or feeling threatened by others. Fear which is not resolved through careful, reasonable investigation leads to states of frustration, desperation, and anxiety. These states produce thoughts (ideas) which direct us to send forth the energy to act out or act against the object(s) of our fear.

As I suggested earlier, problems depend on proper conditions for their existence. Unforgiveness breeds hatred. One of the major problems born from a state of hatred is stress. Stress, improperly managed, gives birth to a host of other problems that emerge and interfere with the quality of life.

CONDITIONS OFTEN CAUSED BY STRESS

Physical and emotional problems that can be associated with or intensified by stress include,

Hypertension or high blood pressure

Various minor muscle twitches and nervous tics

Anxiety

Depression

Headaches

Indigestion

Temporary shortness of breath

Back and neck pain

Tightness in the chest

Gastritis

Menstrual disorders

Irritable bladder

Irritable colon

Some forms of baldness

Worsening of asthmatic conditions

Disturbance of heart rate

Outbreaks of Eczema and Psoriasis

Outbreaks of some viruses

FOOD FOR THOUGHT

In researching this list I was reminded of some wisdom I once shared with a friend who had developed an ulcer that I believe was triggered by many years of suppressed anger and hatred. I said to him, "Ferguson, you must learn not to hate, not even your problems. Don't you know that even the hardest of metals will break when subjected to enough pressure?"

This simple statement must have hit home, because now days when Ferguson notices that I am exhibiting signs of anger, he says to me, "Rob, don't you know that pressure can bust a lead pipe?"

His words always serve to remind me of the damage I am ultimately doing to my physical and mental health. I encourage you to think up some axiom that might be used to help others when you see them being captured by hate. By rescuing a friend, you might motivate that person to throw you a line when it is needed.

Now concerning the ego versus our spiritual instincts, I would like you to consider the following. When we deal with fear from our ego base, we look to our own limited experiences for the answer to our problems. However, when we deal with fear on the basis of our spiritual instincts, we open ourselves to receive direction from a greater source outside of ourselves.

In other words, we can call on God for the power to forgive others. He will give us patience—the type that enables us to forgive others and look for ways to help them. He gives us the power to be still, to be calm, to be reasonable, to be clear-minded, to be forgiving, to be humble, to be just, to be slow to anger, and to be kind. When we are mindful that God's wisdom is available to anyone who asks Him for it (James 1:5), we realize that the knowledge to do the right thing is as near as our own hearts and that hate is nothing but harmful, angry, tragic energy that will have a more negative impact on our lives than any other problem we may be facing.

When we forgive others, we are forgiven for the things we do wrong. That's powerful. Forgiveness is the power to start over and try again. Forgiveness is the power to do it better next time.

To fully enjoy our potential and to increase the potential in others we must learn to forgive ourselves and our fellowman.

There is only one you. There will never be another individual like you in the world again. You have the potential to find your own way and leave a light for others to find their way, too. But if you hate people, you reduce the light of your countenance to a small flicker. And every time you hate someone, you diminish your capacity to regenerate that brightness that your Creator originally gave to you. Love yourself and others through the power of forgiveness, and let your light shine.

HOW TO
SOAR TO SUCCESS

CHAPTER 9

STRENGTHEN YOUR WEAKNESSES

Healthy relationships are found between people whose respect for each other compensates for their weaknesses.

There is something to be said for the old axiom, "Before you can love someone else, you must first learn to love yourself." As we discussed in chapter 7, love is something we receive before we ever do anything to earn it. Love gives us the energy to strengthen our weaknesses. Examples of such encouragement are found during the three most difficult tasks that we undertake in childhood: talking, walking, and reading. Because we were loved in spite of our weaknesses, we had the motivation to take another step. Learning that we are lovable in spite of failure gives us self-respect and keeps us from being seen as a problem by others.

There are two practical ways to achieve self-acceptance and maintain a positive image with others:

1. We need to identify qualities about ourselves that make us lovable in our own opinion, and

2. We need to teach others how we best want to be respected.

The same steps apply to helping other people overcome their belief that they are a problem. They need reassurance that they are lovable, and they may need help identifying what they want from others to secure that reassurance.

Many times when we begin to look for our strengths, we are sidetracked by our weaknesses. Although this tendency is normal, it is important that we focus on our lovable qualities and learn to strengthen our weaknesses in order to move on toward better relationships with others. We can learn the value of self-acceptance and of communicating our needs to others by viewing the progress made toward facilitating people who are physically challenged.

Fortunately, in today's society, major steps are being taken to develop workshops in schools and in the workplace to include perspectives pertinent to individuals who are "differently-abled." The existence of special bathroom fixtures and seating in movie theaters are obvious evidences of the change. Ramps at retail stores, lowered sidewalk curbs, and handicapped parking icons in parking lots all suggest that we are becoming a society that is more aware of and accepting of people who are different from the norm.

All of the apparatus and conveniences that were mentioned above did not come about because of a sudden change of heart on the part of government bureaucrats and those who control industry. It came about because people who are physically challenged led the way with innovation and courage. They overcame negative stereotypes and believed in themselves. Why? Because they first were loved, then learned what was lovable about themselves, then accepted those qualities, and eventually learned ways to teach others how to respect and love them, too. In other words, it was when they stopped perceiving themselves as the problem that they solved their real problems.

LET OTHERS SUCCEED

Twenty-two years ago, when I was attending Boston College, I was taught a valuable lesson by a physically challenged student. I was about to enter a school building when I saw another student in a wheelchair having some difficulty getting through a door. Every time he tried to push the door open wide enough to give time to roll himself out to the street, the door would shut, trapping him in the threshold. I saw this happen to him three times as I hurried up the stairs to assist him.

Immediately upon reaching his position I grabbed the front of his chair with one hand and held the door open with the other. With one quick jerk I pulled him free into the street. Afterwards I stood back, basking in my role as a hero. As we stood there staring at each other, he adjusted his books and repositioned himself in the chair and said rather sharply, "Thank you very much, but I almost had it! A few more tries and I would have made it through!" As I stood there, a bit numb from his reaction, he continued to explain, "Please, I know you meant well, but before you rush to help someone in a wheelchair, ask them if they need your help or ask if there is a way that you could be of assistance."

At first I thought, *How ungrateful of him;* but later that year I underwent spinal surgery for a football related injury, and it was three weeks before I could walk up a flight of stairs. The day I was freed by the doctor to begin exercising, I was preparing to use some equipment in the weight room. I was having some problems bending down to reposition the seat on the stationary bicycle when one of my buddies on the football team hurried over and did it for me.

I knew immediately what that student meant by his words of instruction. I felt helpless, useless, inept, and most importantly, I didn't feel like a whole person. It was as if a part of me was invisible. In that moment I felt like a problem. Maybe that student in the wheelchair at some time in his life felt like one too. But no doubt by learning to identify qualities about himself that he could love and by educating others in how to love him, he empowered himself and separated himself from thinking about himself as a problem. Then he taught others how he preferred to be assisted.

So, from then on I learned to see the physically challenged as whole people. This realization may not have come about as soon in my life had that student not learned the value of loving himself and teaching others how to love and respect him, too. Clearly, in this situation, the teacher appeared and the student showed up.

YOU ARE THE COURSE, BUT ARE YOU TEACHING IT?

When it comes to your own self-worth, you are the course of study and it's your responsibility to teach the course to those with whom you want a lasting relationship. If you don't, people will surely fail at loving you the way you want to be loved. *If you are not willing to be the teacher, don't expect the student to show up.*

I imagine that student in the wheelchair must have overcome many years of stigmatism and patronization. Surely, I was not the first or the last person that he had to instruct in the ways to love and respect him. As I reflect on that situation, I am impressed with his strength and his faith in the human capacity to get past its blissful ignorance. No doubt he was a perfect example of what I classify as a model "FACT Instructor."

A FACT Instructor is someone who perceives how he or she wants to be loved and respected as concrete, factual information. The instructor then communicates these facts to individuals from whom the FACT Instructor wants love and respect.

FACT is the acronym for the qualities the instructor should maintain while teaching others the guidelines to a better relationship with him or her, which are:

FAIRNESS

ACCOUNTABILITY

COURAGE

TRUTH

Almost everyone has room to strengthen themselves in these four virtues. Of course there are other areas of our lives to examine, but in building relationships with others I encourage my communication students to explore the impact of fairness, accountability, courage, and truth in their interaction with others.

STRENGTHEN YOUR LEVEL OF FAIRNESS

FACT Instructors understand and accept certain facts about human relationships. They know that all people are vulnerable to making mistakes and that they, in fact, need to make mistakes in order to learn and grow. Therefore, the instructor understands that the student must be treated with the highest degree of fairness during the instructional process.

Imagine for a moment that you are a student in college who has an instructor that hands out a difficult test on the first day of class before uttering one word of instruction, then tells you that the test will be worth 100 percent of your grade. No doubt you would hate the instructor, because there is no possible way for you to know the answer, in most cases, without first being taught the material.

As absurd as that sounds, we are all guilty of being this type of instructor in our everyday relationships. Evidence of this exists in the clichés that we use to describe how we teach others to love and respect us.

In this next section, I will present some common examples of what I call Astray Clichés, which are familiar phrases that have been given as advice but which lead our students in the wrong direction from how to love and respect us. After each Astray Cliché, I have given a Fact Finder, which are those clear instructional messages that enable students to more accurately locate what makes us feel loved and respected.

Astray Cliché: "Treat people the way *you* want to be treated."

This is the all-time great Astray Cliché. No question, the Golden Rule calls for us to give to others the respect and dignity all of us deserve. But that doesn't mean that the way you want to be treated is exactly the way others want to be treated. We take a lot for granted when we approach relationships with this notion in mind. It could be that you are not offended if a dinner guest does not offer to bring something to your dinner parties, while someone with whom you are now in a relationship grew up with the opposite custom.

Fact Finder: "Treat people the way they say they want to be treated."

If you are the student in a growing relationship, don't be afraid to ask your teacher what is expected of you. Get a clear understanding in the beginning of what your teacher's relationship policies are and how you can achieve the highest grade.

Astray Cliché: "Love means never having to say that you're sorry."

You can't count the number of people who felt disrespected or have seen their relationship destroyed because their partner believed in this misleading advice. First, the cliché is ambiguous. Does it mean that the one who loves is not capable of doing something for which they should feel sorry? We all know that this is not possible for human beings in the real world. Or does it suggest that because one loves, that he or she shouldn't have to apologize? Even in instances where both parties know that each other is wrong, people deny the truth.

FAIRNESS SECURES RELATIONSHIPS THAT LAST

The Beat Generation standup comedian, Lenny Bruce, once said, "Even if your wife catches you in the act of adultery, deny it!" When you deny treating someone unfairly, you signal that you don't value the other person's right to fairness. Consequently you insult the intelligence of the other person. No healthy relationship was ever built on denial. It's important to remember the comedian was joking! Add fairness to the mortar of any relationship that you want to endure the test of time.

Fact Finder: "Love is being able to say that you are sorry."

Love inspires you to say that you are sorry. Saying that you are sorry is the start of the healing process. By uttering those words you show humility and respect for the rights of the others whom you may have offended, and you provide them a way to become strengthened, ironically, so that they can forgive you.

A good friend of mine told me that he and his wife had not been married long when he apologized for offending her with a comment. Later that week his wife mentioned to him that she had shared the incident with her mother. Her mother informed her that she should be very happy because she had a good man. She agreed, but she quizzed her mother about why she thought so. Her mother replied, "Because in thirty years of marriage your father has never said he was sorry about anything. Couples can overcome almost anything when they can apologize to one another."

STRENGTHEN YOUR ACCOUNTABILITY

A FACT Instructor is accountable to the course values. The best way for FACT Instructors to develop trusting relationships with their students is to make the course values clear from the beginning and stay accountable to them. While it is understood that the student is to adhere to the values, the consistency with which the instructor upholds the values is how the student will measure his or her success.

It is also important that the instructor does not change the values of the course too often or without informing the student that they have been changed. For example, suppose one of your course values is:

"Please call me if you are going to be late meeting me for our date."

When the student shows up an hour late, it would not be fair to the student if you did not inform that person that he or she had not met the stated values of the course. By not letting the student know that the course's values about promptness had been overlooked, you signal that the stated values have changed and, more importantly, that they are not to be taken seriously.

Likewise, "If you talk the talk, then you must walk the walk." In other words, make sure that you call if you are going to be late for your meetings as well. There is no quicker way to destroy the morale of students taking your course than for you to go astray from your own stated values. Remember, students are always watching you. It's what you do, not what you say, that counts.

STRENGTHEN YOUR LEVEL OF COURAGE

Success as a FACT Instructor will depend on an ability to express courage in two critical human emotional levels—vulnerability and patience.

Level one—vulnerability: No true expression of love or desire for love and respect can be communicated or experienced unless we are courageous enough to disengage from feelings of fear.

Our hesitancy to share information about how we best want to be treated by others comes from two sources:1) our fear that people will think that we are too controlling, or 2) our feeling that others will think we are too self-absorbed. If we are hesitant to let others know our needs, we are too concerned with being criticized for loving ourselves. In building healthy relationships between two people, both must be willing to love themselves with confidence and to celebrate that fact with the other person.

It is loving ourselves unashamedly that gives us the courage to let others see our lovable traits and communicate our valid needs to them. People who are stuck in their emotionally confused state of low self-esteem or self-doubt may respond to us with arrows of envy at first. The people with whom we are trying to build relationships may feel disjointed from their own self-love power which may disable them from loving us the way we have requested.

The other person's self-doubt may keep him or her from responding the way we were hoping for. But in our ability to love ourselves, we can keep offenses and disappointments from wounding us. This is why our own level of courage must be strong. We put ourselves in a vulnerable position when we ask for respect, and people may not give us what we ask for; but if we never ask, we have a narrow chance of improving our relationship.

Unfortunately, some people consider others to be too controlling if they provide a clear direction to the way of their heart. If they see us as controlling they will not want to win our hearts, no matter how clear the path to it may be. To avoid this destructive dynamic, we must be careful not to withhold respect from others even while waiting for respect in return.

People who ignore clear explanations of what we want in a relationship are the people who are not interested in learning to love and respect others in their own way. These are the ones who act like relationship experts, ignoring our instructions and suggesting that we don't know how to teach our own course.

While we must have the courage to say what we want, we must also have equal courage to drop certain students from the course, no matter how attractive their transcripts might appear. People who don't enjoy being around us when our self-love is showing are the same ones who are slow to lend an ear to hear about our promotions, graduations, raises, and victories. They would rather hear about the tragedy and sorrow in our life. These students may never pass the course, but we shouldn't relinquish the right to teach it to them. Remember, you are the only one who knows how you can best be loved.

No One Can Teach
Your Course Better Than You

It is an unfortunate reality that a person who loves himself and who is willing to celebrate his virtues with others may be envied by those who are filled with self-doubt. The doubter may accuse the one who has found self-love of being self-absorbed. All humankind is in pursuit of peace and harmony with self, and self-confidence will be envied by those who don't know how to find it themselves. But neither peace nor harmony with self can be achieved unless one can accept oneself as God has made him or her and learn to love what God has made of him or her.

Individuals must learn to love themselves unconditionally the way their parents loved them when they were first born. It is this power of self-love that FACT Instructors share and celebrate with each other. Anyone who sees them as self-absorbing are people who desire the confidence that the instructors have but who haven't learned to embrace their own potential.

Level two—patience: FACT Instructors have learned what it means to have patience towards their relationship students, and most importantly they appreciate the ecstatic results.

I often facilitate small group discussions on relationships where I suggest the principle that they teach another person how they best want to be treated. Too often someone in the group responds, "If I teach him, then that will take all the fun out of it." All I can say is, "Then don't complain about how bad the food tastes when he tries to cook your favorite meal without your secret sauce."

People who feel hesitant about teaching others how they want to be treated believe that their relationship will become too predictable and leave little anticipation of surprise. But what they are really saying by not explaining their needs is, "I am not really interested in experiencing how I best want to be loved and respected."

People need not fear the loss of spontaneity in a relationship after teaching another person the art of loving them. To the contrary, instructing someone else is part of the loving process. Effective instruction is spontaneous in its process. It is in this uncontrolled setting where both the teacher and the student realize that an understanding has transpired, that the goose bumps should occur for both of them.

The teacher has achieved actualization, because he or she has successfully gifted a portion of his or herself to the student. The student, by allowing the knowledge to be impregnated, provides it a place to grow and take new forms of expression. Those new forms and styles of expression bring the ecstatic results that FACT Instructors learn to love and appreciate.

A clear example of this is in the situation of parents rearing children. When we teach our children the many different ways to love and respect us, we do not do so by fearing that we will become bored or disinterested in their expressions of love for us. Once our children understand our expectations, they have unique ways of expressing their love that surprise us. It is only when we force them to use our form and style that we run into trouble, because what we experience in those instances is their awkward attempts to mimic us. Trying to contrive how the needs are met will lead to frustration on the part of the student and leave a dull experience for the teacher.

PRACTICING PATIENCE REAPS REWARDS

Successful relationships are not achieved without patience. Patience means that you must sometimes create new ways to instruct your students, because not all people learn the same way. It may take a while before you understand the student's best learning style, so don't hesitate to ask about the way they best learn new information. Some people learn visually, some kinesthetically, and others audibly.

Some students learn better through art forms (sculpture, paintings, music, and dance), others through different game formats and scientific explorations; still others have their learning accelerated by intellectual approaches (deep conversation, reading out loud, listening to experts). However, in order to learn and master the material, all students need to know that their instructors will be patient with them as long as they are willing to continue trying to learn.

The next virtue that FACT Instructors should strengthen themselves in, after Fairness, Accountability, and Courage, is Truth. We will explore the importance of Truth in the next chapter. FACT Instructors know that the amalgam of these four qualities brings a cohesive power into the wide variety of relationships we have with others.

You will strengthen the bonds you have with others as you establish fair guidelines, are accountable to the boundaries that you set, and have courage to tell others what you need from them. As you instruct them in meeting your needs, you also teach them how to speak up for their own needs. These truths will protect you from damaging disappointments and will free you to enjoy each other.

CHAPTER 10

OPTIMIZE YOUR STRENGTHS

Truth is above all things.

Truth is a strength available to all people. Knowing the truth of your own strengths will help you advance faster than knowing facts about your weaknesses. Facts describe the events that take place between people, but truth describes the motives and the intent of the heart during the action. Wise FACT Instructors have learned that knowing the truth concerning someone's intentions will advance a relationship faster than knowing facts that describe what someone did.

Truth has the power to free you from disappointments and frustrations. Whenever you begin to feel discouraged, take time to ask yourself, "What is the truth in this situation?" Perhaps, for example, you didn't get invited to participate in something. When you determine the truth, you may discover that even if you had been asked, you honestly would have preferred having your time free for something else. Perhaps the truth was that it was only an oversight that your name was excluded. God has promised that truth is always a safe shelter in which we are free to enjoy His greater plan for us as we learn to trust Him.

A dramatic illustration of this is a story I was told of a young married couple who often fished and camped with friends. On one occasion the husbands were to go out a day ahead of the wives who would join them for lunch on the second day. As the time neared, one of the husbands decided he didn't want his wife to make the long trip to join them for such a brief time. She was hurt and couldn't understand this unexpected reversal of plans. He didn't give her a further reason, and she suffered disappointment from his decision.

The afternoon that she was to have been at the lake, her father, who drove a gasoline tanker, was in a dangerous accident where his trailer turned over, spilling 8500 gallons of gasoline onto the highway. Seeing flames, he ran from the truck just in time to hear deadly explosions behind him, escaping with only a small burn on one leg. Within minutes, traffic reporters were alerting drivers to stay away from the area, and the young wife heard the news of her father's accident.

Sobbing with hysteria, she was able to drive to the scene of the accident to find her father safely watching the firemen fight the flames. He greatly appreciated her offer to take him home. A few hours later she came to realize how glad she was that her husband had decided that she should not join him at the lake. She would have been full of regret to learn that her father had been alone through his trauma. This truth kept her from being angry at her husband.

One cannot be a FACT Instructor without committing to some of the principles associated with truth, for any instruction developed and administered without truth in its mortar will end in failure for both the student and the instructor.

Truth is accuracy. As we stated earlier, know the way to your own heart. A helpful exercise to find the truth and reach your heart is to first develop a list of ten verbs that best represent why you love yourself. Verbs are the purest of all words in the English language. They take you closer to the *real* you than any other words can.

Your list may include such words as:

act	believe
appreciate	build
aspire	cause

compel	laugh
create	launch
cry	learn
dance	listen
delight	model
dream	move
embrace	need
encourage	notice
engineer	nurture
entertain	object
explore	obtain
feel	organize
finance	pardon
follow	play
forgive	produce
generate	promise
give	promote
heal	receive
help	relate
hope	remember
identify	resolve
inspire	safeguard

serve	vegetate
shout	verge
sing	warm
talk	watch
teach	yearn
team	yield
travel	yoke
understand	zip
unify	zoom
validate	

What Kind of Verb Are You?

Don't apply adverbs to modify or evaluate your descriptive verbs. In this phase of identifying your love for yourself, you do not need to be distracted by personal opinions and judgments of how you perform these verbs.

Judgment does not say what you are; it says what is good or bad, right or wrong about what you are. Verbs, on the other hand, are tools of description. They enable you to define your true feelings and observations about your behavior and physical image. Once you have developed your list, share it with your students. Inform them in what ways the verbs best represent why you love yourself.

A healthy pattern for this important discussion with those who are learning how to love you follows:

1. Clearly state the verb by using it in a sentence that illustrates why you love yourself. If one of the verbs that you chose is *Share,* you might say, "I love myself because I have a great capacity to share with others." This should signal to your students that one of the best ways to love and respect you is to share with you and to allow you to reciprocate the act of sharing.

2. Describe what the verb means to you. Talk about some of the different feelings that occur in you when you think about your relationship with the verb. Remember, do not make judgments or opinions about yourself or your verb.

3. Discuss what it felt like as you developed your list of verbs. What process did you undertake in order to complete the list? Was it difficult, or did the descriptive verbs come to mind quickly? This signals to the student how sincere and clear you are about why you love and respect yourself.

4. Explain what it has meant for you to be able to describe to yourself—why you love and respect

yourself; i.e., how you felt before and after you developed the list.

Don't ask the students to evaluate the list, simply give instructions to share with you what the words mean to them. Then ask them to create a personal list to share with you, so that you can become aware of what your students love about themselves. Tell them what you think their verbs mean. In each case, make sure to correct them if either is inaccurate in understanding the true meaning of the verbs as they are intended to be used.

TRUTH IS REALITY

No one can expect more from you than the truth. And once you have shared the truth about how you want to be loved and respected, you stand in the bright light of "self-love reality." Self-love reality is a perception of what it is that you love and respect about yourself, separate from any interpretations given to you by others or any evaluative language you used to think about yourself in the process.

You may find it difficult at first to have a self-love reality because so much of our self-love perception is based on evaluations that others have expressed towards us. Very little of what we think is lovable about ourselves comes from our own non-judgmental voice. Whenever we talk about our lovable qualities, we often relate in either descriptive adjectives or with modifying adverbs to explain how well or poorly we did something. Neither adjectives nor adverbs describe our inner essence, which is that human being who exists when no one else is watching and when we have stopped performing just to please others.

Jesus was once challenged on the laws of God by religious leaders of his time. Jesus' response to them confirmed this necessary act of self-love.

> Then one of them, *which was* a lawyer, asked *him a question*, tempting him, and saying,
>
> Master, which *is* the great commandment in the law?
>
> Jesus said unto him, Thou shalt love the Lord thy God with all thy heart, and with all thy soul, and with all thy mind.
>
> This is the first and great commandment.
>
> And the second *is* like unto it, Thou shalt love thy neighbour as thyself.
>
> On these two commandments hang all the law and the prophets.
>
> Matthew 22:35-40 KJV

It is not egotistical to love yourself. In fact, it is one of the two greatest commandments from God. We must love ourselves before we can truly love others. Once we know how to be good to ourselves, we understand how to be good to others. This self-love reality is vital to the growth of healthy relationships. Years of asking college students to list self-descriptive verbs and share with their classmates why they love themselves produced two profound discoveries:

1. Too many of them could not identify themselves with the use of verbs. They did not have the ability to think about themselves in a clear, descriptive manner that is available through the use of verbs. They were better equipped to describe their external image with adjectives than to explain their internal essence with verbs.

2. As students were able to develop lists of verbs to describe themselves, I could see a growing confidence in their sense of themselves.

Your students will respond to your lovable qualities with the same enthusiasm that you demonstrate to them. If you are positive and excited about your list of verbs, your student will be positive, too. If you are listless, hesitant, and unsure, your student will doubt if you really know why others should respect you.

Any good instructor knows, if you are not in love with and excited about the course you are teaching, you can't expect your students to be excited. When it comes to winning the respect of others, you are the teacher, you are the course, and you are the reward for the person who passes the test. Always strive to teach the course with love for yourself and your students in mind. Know that in order to be a successful FACT Instructor you must know your material and be true to your course. Above all, remember that no one can teach others how to respect you better than you can.

CHAPTER 11

ACKNOWLEDGE THOSE WHO HELP YOU

None of us were born with eyes in the back of our heads.

How many of us can cut our own hair with confidence and feel impressed with the finished product? Furthermore, which one of us has ever sat in a barber or hair stylist's chair and viewed the back of our heads without using a mirror? Those who can answer in the affirmative are people born with eyes in the back of their heads—an unlikely scenario.

No matter how sophisticated we become as a species, we still find ourselves dependent on others to help us with the simple trivialities of everyday living. Where projecting and maintaining our image is concerned, we find our greatest reliance on others. Whoever said that "reality is ninety percent perception" really knew what he was talking about. Why? Because people spend a great deal of time trying to project and maintain their images before others.

How people dress, behave, walk, and talk is greatly shaped by how people want others to perceive them. Therefore, getting some feedback about the image they cast is very important. It is so important that people have, over time, discovered many methods for checking the appropriateness of their appearance.

For example, before we had mirrors, people would check if they were projecting an acceptable image by looking into a calm body of water with a murky bottom, or into a piece of silver, flat and smoothly polished. They would look to see if they had applied their makeup properly, or if their hair was arranged neatly and their beards trimmed evenly. They checked to make sure their clothing fit appropriately, and to make sure that all the colors matched and met the social criteria for correctness.

It is of such importance to people to project the correct physical image, that they sometimes risk their own safety and that of others to do so. Nothing serves this point better than the practice of some to groom themselves in their automobiles. Some would "chalk it up to vanity," but I suggest that it has more to do with the pressure to keep up with social standards than mere vanity. The fear is that the perception others have of our physical appearance might somehow equate to our competence, reliability, and decency.

On one particular occasion, I was driving behind a female motorist who swerved from lane to lane, making her way through the early morning traffic, oblivious to the danger she was creating all around her. I was amazed by her determination as she teased her hair and applied her eyeliner, mascara, rouge, and lipstick. It was obviously important to her.

Occasionally she looked up to check her image in the rear view mirror, then lowered her head again in order to apply more makeup using her small hand-held mirror. In all, the process took place for approximately four to five miles. Even when she had finished the job, she continued to fuss with her hair in the rear view mirror.

Women aren't the only offenders. One day I followed a man who shaved and put on his tie while driving. This took place on one of the busiest freeways in northern California. Though he used an electric razor, the maneuver required him to steer the car with his knees!

There are times when people have very little control in assuring that their image is up to par. That is when we turn to others for help. Society has created and agreed on certain forms of feedback to be used to help us manage our images. In each case, we depend on others to provide a much-needed service because none of us possesses an extra pair of eyes, without which we are likely to project an unwanted image.

THE NOISE OF YOUR JUDGMENTAL VOICE

So much do we depend on others to help us stay in check that when we discover they have failed to do so, we respond with an array of emotions. It's as if part of us gets terribly embarrassed, while at the same time another part of us feels disappointed in the person who could have helped us but didn't.

Have you ever had dinner with strangers and learned later that you had accidentally smeared food on your nose? If so, you will know where I'm headed with this. Let's assume the meal has been over for quite awhile and you have been engaged in an intense conversation with these people for the last ten to fifteen minutes. Suddenly nature calls and you excuse yourself. In the restroom, you get a glimpse of yourself in the mirror and notice that your nose is smeared with whipped cream that got away from you while you were polishing off your chocolate cream pie during dessert.

What would your response be? Most people would answer this way, "How could they let me sit there all that time with whipped cream on my nose?"

The question implies that we have an expectation of others in a situation such as this that was not met by the strangers in this example. And yet, what communication have we had with them to imply that we welcome their interaction on such a critical and sensitive level? Probably none! Remember, we're dealing with strangers here.

Not all people are ready to be told in front of others that there is a noticeable flaw with their image, i.e., whipped cream on the nose. Some would want to be told in secret. Therefore, most people will treat you the way they would want to be treated in such a situation. Some people will attempt to cue you that your image is out of whack by gesturing or gently touching that part of the body or clothing, in the hope that you will become aware of the offensive object without being told.

Braver souls may whisper in your ear or scribble a note on a napkin. And there are those who would feel perfectly comfortable wiping it off themselves. The majority, however, would rather play it safe and let you find out on your own. Maybe you feel they have violated some higher order by doing so. Instead, they may simply be saying, "Having whipped cream on your nose ain't no big deal, you are acceptable to me, whipped cream and all."

Each of these people has your best interest at heart, and undoubtedly, all have had your problem at some time. The important thing is not to come back to the table feeling as if these people have broken your trust or that you have done something which casts doubt on your social graces. All this will do is create a dialogue in your head that will interfere with your openness to the people and their interesting histories.

This internal dialogue creates a type of psychological noise which disrupts your ability to hear and retain the information provided for you by the others at the table. That information could be anything from how to earn a commission on a sale to a great stock tip. It might be the announcement that a great cellist is coming to town or a medical breakthrough that could save your life or the life of someone you love.

When you become preoccupied with your own "voice of judgment," the noise can become so loud and absorbing that it forces you to stop listening to everyone else. You will no doubt continue to hear the sound of the conversation going on at the table, but you will probably stop listening. There is a distinct difference between the two. Hearing is the involuntary response to sounds that occur outside your body, somewhere in the environment. Drop a book on the floor. Unless you are hearing impaired, you will hear this sound. Hearing is an involuntary reflex.

Listening, on the other hand, requires intent, with the single purpose of understanding what you are hearing. The sound of the book hitting the floor is not a sound that you listen to with intent. Therefore, you apply no special meaning to it.

When a "voice of judgment" causes you to tune out the conversation of the others at the table, their words become much like the sound the book makes when it hits the floor. While you can hear it, you don't listen to it with any special intent, and as a result you fail to benefit from the meaning in the messages.

I Apologize, My Image Got in the Way

We depend on no other set of eyes more than those of our significant others to assist us in managing our social appearance. While we are disappointed when strangers fail to inform us of a smudge on our face, or pepper in our teeth, we seldom let them know of our feeling of bewilderment. The opposite is true when we discover that our significant others have failed to inform us that our image is somehow marred. Not only do we let them know that we are disappointed in their failure to inform us that something about our image was out place, we often make the unhealthy attempt to blame them for our feelings of a "diminished self" that we carry about ourselves.

One critical social situation where we strive to be at our best is the job interview. We can become so concerned, both as receivers and senders of images, that our entire emotional disposition can be altered if we discover after an interview that we did not appear the way we thought we did.

I found myself between jobs some years ago. I was thirty-one, my wife twenty-two, and we had been married for about three years and had a two-year-old son. We also had a new house and our first mortgage. I had just left a position as an assistant manager of distributions for a company in San Francisco. It was a job I could no longer tolerate. So with the agreement of my wife, I quit.

Despite the fact that I had a BA in communication from Boston College and was close to completing my graduate work at San Francisco State University, I found it tough to find work. Wherever I went, I was told that I was either over or under qualified. Six months had passed since I left my previous job and our savings were depleted. I found myself borrowing from relatives to make ends meet. I was desperate to find employment.

Finally someone responded to my resumé by phone. That person arranged for me to come into the office the next morning for a formal interview. The next day, I got up bright and early, shaved, put on my best outfit and made sure that my shoes had a spit shine. I looked in the mirror and checked to see if every hair was in place. (Well, at least those that I still had left.) To my eye, everything seemed to be in order. Next, I went into the kitchen where my wife was preparing breakfast for herself and our son. From a distance and in a hurried voice I said, "Honey, check me out." Then I did a pirouette.

Looking over her shoulder she said, "You look good to me."

With that, I kissed her and my son and rushed out. I felt I looked good and that the day was my prize, not only for looking my best which I thought should be enough, but also for being my best.

I approached the interview with an air of confidence, and was amazed to find that every question asked was one I had anticipated. I felt I answered each one creatively and concisely. As the interview continued, my confidence grew.

Soon I could feel my power surging, especially when the interviewer began to express ways in which he could identify with me. The school he attended in New Hampshire was the arch rival of the school I had attended. He mentioned a keen interest in public speaking and I was able to share with him some of the cutting-edge concepts I had learned in graduate school.

Finally, he identified himself as a fan of professional football and the New Orleans Saints, the team I had played for in the seventies. Everything seemed to be going my way. He then suggested that I go with him to meet some of the other managers and supervisors to whom I would be reporting. They all seemed like pleasant people and received me well. I kept thinking it was my day. As the interview was coming to an end, I felt confident about my chances of getting the job. I left the interview and walked out into the bright afternoon sunlight. It really did feel like a perfect day.

And then the unthinkable happened. As I walked down California Street, I caught a glimpse of my reflection in a store window and I didn't like what I saw. As I moved closer to the window to get a better look, I discovered that the back of my blazer and slacks was covered with lint balls.

I had used a lint brush to groom the front of my clothing, but in the excitement I had failed to do the same to the back of my outfit. As the significance of my discovery dawned on me, I felt my confidence lift away from me like helium in the air. I felt the rigid coldness of panic in my chest and face and for a few moments, I was riveted to my image reflecting back at me from the store window. Within seconds, my judgmental voice sang a loser's song. What I had perceived earlier as the interviewer's identification with me, now seemed to be nothing more than the general congeniality extended to all candidates. I reasoned that the managers who seemed so interested a few minutes before were probably now convinced that I lacked the attention to detail necessary for the job.

SELF-FOCUS FEEDS FAILURE

During the hour-long ride home, I was overwhelmed by a mounting sense of failure and rejection. By the time I walked into the house, I felt like a microwaved hot dog approaching one minute past done.

The veins were bulging from my neck and my eyes were full of tears of anguish as my wife greeted me with a wide-eyed, "How did it go? How do you think you did?"

Trying to be as calm as possible, I said, "Why did you let me go out of the house with lint all over the back of my clothes? If I can't count on you to do something as simple as that, then I'm in real trouble. There's no way they are going to hire me to be a doorman at that hotel when I can't even groom myself properly."

Her response startled me. "I can barely see the lint on your clothes. Those people at the hotel probably couldn't see it either." When she said those words I felt a small portion of my strength return to my body.

I hadn't been home two hours, still quietly brooding and distant, when the phone rang. To my amazement, it was the manager at the Stanford Court calling to offer me the job as doorman and suggest that I start work that weekend. Ironically, one of the things he said they look for most is the doorman candidate's sense of presentation, cleanliness, grooming, and style, and that they were convinced I demonstrated all of these at the highest level.

When I hung up the phone, I apologized to my wife and let her know that I had been accepted for the job. I also apologized to myself and to God, because in that three hour period I had abandoned both faith in myself and in my most precious resource, the unwaning support and grace of my Lord and Savior, Jesus Christ. I had abandoned my trust in Him to work things out for me, yet I had been blessed in spite of my doubt.

Indoctrinated most of my life by a poor economic community, I lived with the felt need to appear prosperous. Image was everything. Therefore, whenever my image was marred in any way, I could not help but believe that there was something wrong with my character, my abilities, and to some degree, my destiny. *How could a person with ragged clothing, or a dirty house and second-hand furniture have a worthwhile destiny or meaningful dreams?* I reasoned.

Feeling good about the way we look is healthy for the maintenance of a solid self-esteem. We naturally feel better about ourselves when we are meeting our own expectations and the standards set for us by certain individuals in our lives. It is foolish to believe that there will ever be a culture or civilization that doesn't have some general standard of acceptability with which we strive to comply.

What we must reach for is the acceptance of those whose images do not comply with our own. People are not the problem when their appearance differs from our own. For every person whose image deviates from the norm, there will be a much greater number who are anxious to comply. Both are fine.

However, we must develop more tolerance for those who desire to express their individuality. We must reach down into our unused reservoir of patience and see that all human beings feel welcomed. Applying pressure to the few non-conformists only causes those who are already conforming to become more fixated on maintaining and further shaping their images to fit the very standard they already approximate. It is my belief that those who resist the norm are not doing so out of rebellion, but rather because of the frustration and anxiety that come from feeling that they are unable to meet the standard.

There will always be those who hear a different tune, dance a different dance, and laugh at the same joke but for a different reason. There will always be those who wear their hair differently and match their clothing unconventionally.

No matter how, or in what way, we are different from one another, we must always remember that we are each the other's keeper. And because none of us has eyes in the back of his head, we are all vulnerable. Therefore, it is wise to be kind to others, regardless of the physical image they project. For all we know, it might be those very people on whom we ultimately rely to help us preserve the image we hold dear.

WHEN THE DOORMAN SAVED THE DAY

While I was attending graduate school at San Francisco State, I worked as a doorman at the Stanford Court Hotel, a five-star hotel on San Francisco's famous Nob Hill. From my post, I witnessed just how important it is to people that others be willing to help them keep their images up to par.

Since the doorman is often the first person guests see when they arrive, the hotel depended on me to provide the best possible service. Though many guests took the time to commend me and the hotel, others seemed to find me an appropriate target for their anger or frustrations. I can't count the number of times I welcomed guests to the hotel who treated me like a door*mat*, instead of a door*man*.

On one occasion, a high-powered executive was delivered to the hotel by his chauffeur. I opened his door and greeted him with a smile and said, "Good afternoon, Sir! Welcome to the Stanford Court Hotel. I trust all is well. I will tag your luggage and have it delivered to your room. Please allow me a moment to identify your bags and give you the corresponding stubs."

Before I could move to count his bags, he tore into me. "I don't need any stubs! Just make sure my bags find their way to my room!"

"Sir," I replied, "I will make it my business to see that your bags arrive at your room. If one of the front desk staff should inquire about the whereabouts of your stubs, please inform him that the doorman will pass them on to the bell person. Thank you and enjoy your stay with us."

As he walked away I thought to myself, *What in the world is bothering him?* At the same time, I could feel my blood pressure rising. For the first time I felt like giving a guest a piece of my mind, but even back then I believed that people were not the problem. Besides, my mother had always taught me to respond to anger with kindness.

Later that evening, one of the bell staff informed me that Mr. Executive would be coming down soon and would need a taxi. An unexpected meeting had been called and he had already dismissed his chauffeur for the day.

When he came to the front door, I had already whistled for a cab and had it waiting for him. As he moved to step into the taxi, I noticed that his jacket collar and shirt were badly disarranged. When he arrived earlier in the day, the executive was impeccably dressed and everything was coordinated and arranged as if he had just stepped out of the pages of GQ magazine. Put aside any ill feelings I had for the executive and let my instincts take over I said, "Have a good meeting sir. Just a second, let me help you with your collars." Within a second, I had helped him make the necessary adjustments. For a fraction of a moment, he stood there, speechless. Then he said, "Thanks. I really appreciate that," and climbed into the taxi.

I was just finishing my shift when he returned from his meeting. "Excuse me, could I have a word with you?" the executive asked, as he motioned for me.

"Sir, I was on my way home for the evening, but I can spare a moment. I would really like to get home in time to spend a few minutes with my kids before they go to sleep."

"It will only take a moment," he interjected. "I really appreciated what you did for me tonight."

"And what was that, sir?" I asked.

"Helping with my collar the way you did, I really thought that was special," he answered. With a sincere tone in his voice and expression on his face, he reached out and shook my hand. "I was on my way to a very important meeting, with people I had never met before. It was important for me to make a good first impression. In the twenty years I have been in business, I have found that people often base their decisions on the most trivial things."

Before he checked out of the hotel, Mr. Executive left me a $50 tip and a very nice thank you letter that I have kept to remind me that people are never the problem.

CHAPTER 12

REJOICE WHEN OTHERS SUCCEED

Sometimes you must sacrifice what you like for who you love.

There is no greater success in life than to help others enjoy the fullness of what life has to offer them. I call it God's Great Investment Plan. When we invest our time and love in others, we are guaranteed a return of having our same needs met. Galatians 6:2&7 KJV says, **"Bear ye one another's burdens, and so fulfil the law of Christ. . . . Be not deceived; God is not mocked: for whatsoever a man soweth, that shall he also reap."** If we treat others with respect, we will reap respect. If we act with love towards others, we will be loved.

The young door-to-door salesman, mentioned in Chapter One, told my friend that he was pressured by his peers to rebel against education. Kids who were "soft" were taken advantage of by the other kids. If a student turned in homework and made a good grade, he or she was accused of trying to make the other kids look stupid. Anyone who impressed the teacher was taunted and terrified by the kids who saw following rules as a weakness.

He said that getting an education was difficult because of peer pressure, and before he was sixteen, he had been in trouble with authorities many times. The people who owned the magazine sales company found him "hangin' out" on the streets and said, "Let us teach you how to work for a living and discover your potential." They trained him, prayed with him, and found great pleasure in teaching him how to succeed on his own. Their company wasn't about selling magazines, it was about helping both their employees and their customers find a better life.

Understanding Softens The Heart For Learning

It is not always easy to help someone else succeed. It seems impossible to teach someone whose heart is hard; especially when their ears go deaf, their soul turns cold, their reasoning skills become unreasonable. If the person you are trying to help or instruct has a hardened heart, you may need to soften their exterior with understanding before they are ready to learn.

As a public speaker, I often give talks to students in inner-city schools. Too often, I notice that it takes teachers an extra fifteen minutes to get the attention of certain students. While the majority of students are prepared to hear the message, a few will ignore my presence and their teacher's request to pay attention. With downcast eyes and rigid torsos, they turn their bodies and their attention away from me.

On most occasions, I rescue the teachers by saying, "It's okay, let them sit where they wish. My voice is strong and I am sure that he or she can hear me from there." I make this concession because I believe I understand why these children are behaving in this manner. Their hearts are hardened.

Most of the time a hardened heart comes from a lack of trust. Maybe this trust deficit is the result of being constantly disappointed in the way a person feels he or she has been treated by others. Or perhaps it comes from the nagging suspicion that in the end, his or her efforts will always result in failure. Perhaps the student is afraid to feel the excitement of goose bumps, believing that disappointment will soon follow. It could also come because a person is afraid of his or her feelings, or because that person is anxious to maintain some sense of control over his or her environment.

In the mind of someone who lives in a world of chaos and betrayal, it is difficult to believe that paying attention to a teacher or speaker could bring rewards. Trust requires opening the door to one's heart, and lowering the veil to show the real person inside. A sensitive person can be frightened by this vulnerability, especially if they have been punished in the past for such emotional exposure.

I understand the fear these people live with and therefore, I am prepared to meet them where they are emotionally. In fact, I believe there is a better chance of reaching them with the seed of truth when they are allowed to preserve the control they seem to cherish. For these students, this moment of being in control may be the only time in the day that they feel empowered.

It is quite rational for any person to want to protect himself or herself from hurt. The act of protecting oneself, however, often causes the wound that hardens the heart so that it cannot receive the seeds of knowledge and love. That is the nature of the dilemma. For while we must open up to receive, we do so to a world that has already caused us pain and disappointment.

A HEART IS LIKE THE SOIL

I have found through my own trials that it helps to understand that I am not alone in my pain. Every person I come in contact with has also experienced pain and disappointment in some form. In some way we are all afraid, hesitant, and looking for conditions that might be harmful. But we must also learn not to shut out the world, for when we do, we deprive ourselves of the many loving and joyful people and events that make life a gift to embrace.

Each time I am able to share my message with students, I tell them the story Jesus taught of the sower who scattered seed along his path. In the parable, some seed fell on hard, rocky places and did not survive when the hot sun came up. Seed that fell in thorny places full of weeds eventually were choked out. But when the seed fell on good (soft and fertile) soil, it produced an abundant crop—as many as a hundred times what had been planted.

I challenge them with these words, "Imagine your heart is soil and the words I have come to share with you are the seeds that will be planted in you to grow food—food that you can live on, food that will feed your families, or food that is stored for use when famine comes to the land.

"Suppose that the seeds I give you will grow trees, and suppose that once you eat the fruit of those trees, you will have the strength you need to accept challenges without the fear of failure and build relationships with people without walls of criticism between you. Suppose that this fruit will fortify you and enable you to withstand the false judgments of those who attack you out of ignorance and insecurity. And suppose that this fruit will enable you to love yourself and celebrate your existence and proclaim your place in this world as unique and purposeful."

Then I tell them that the seed I have come to plant in them is a seed of hope. I share with them that at the age of fourteen, I could neither read nor count beyond the fourth grade level. Nor could I accurately tell time by looking at the dials on the face of a clock. I tell them that I have suffered under the supervision of teachers who had no interest in my education and no skills to reach me at my depth of despair.

As I speak these words, the room always becomes silent. Where there once was clambering and whispering, silence reigns and wide eyes signal a heightened sense of interest. Their fascination is triggered by the distinction between what I am saying and the image they had of me when I arrived, that of a football hero and university professor.

What they come to realize and find most inspiring is that my life before the professional success was much like their own and in some cases worse. They learn that a tree will indeed grow from the seed when it is allowed to grow in the soil of their hearts, and that the tree will produce the fruit of hope—hope that when an effort is made, opportunities will come. They are learning that nothing good comes from being too aggressive, too passive, or too hardened.

SOMEONE IS READY TO FOLLOW YOU

I let them know that someone is always watching to see if they will do the right thing in any given situation. I also tell them that someone already sees them as leaders. Since there are people following them, I ask them how they plan to handle their responsibility of leadership. Will they be careful how they live their lives? I ask if they have considered where they will lead those who are following them.

I want them to know and understand that they are not the problem, and I want them to see that no matter what they have done or what others have said about them, they are not the cause of the problems in the world. Every problem they have encountered, been a part of, or felt defeated by, was in the world long before they came along. Most of all, I want them to know that they have the power within themselves to overcome any problem or challenge that confronts them.

At this point, I always ask the students how they would feel about having this seed planted in them, and without exception, they express their willingness to nurture the seed. Even those students who were resistant in the beginning are eager to receive. They are always excited when I tell them that if they have been listening from the beginning of my presentation, they have already received the seed. If it took them awhile to settle in their seat, I explain to them, they may have only received a portion of the message. Therefore, it may take longer for some seed to take root, depending on how hard the soil of their hearts has become.

If their hearts are hard, it will take longer before they can eat from the tree. They understand the principle that it is possible for the hard soil to receive a seed. But it takes the seed much longer to germinate, for the seedling has a harder time working its way through the hard soil in search of the nutrients it needs to help it grow. The soil of our hearts needs to be watered with truth in order to receive the seeds that make us grow.

When I finish my presentation, many of the students follow me out of the auditorium and ask me questions about the idea of strength in softness. I explain it to them this way: being soft is being able to accept life for what it has to offer. The key word here is "accept." I remind them that the soil that makes up the entire planet, whether it is the soil at the bottom of the deepest ocean or that which exists in the crevices of the highest mountain peak, awaits the arrival of the seed so that it can show its greatness. The soil must be soft if the seed is to reach its greatest potential; and the soil is at its best when it is nurturing the seed, because that is what it was created to do. In other words, true greatness comes when the soil of our hearts is soft enough to receive others, *as they are, where they are, and for what purpose they exist.*

During these chat sessions, I often notice one student who remains seated on the sidelines. When the questions have all been asked and the others have gone on their way, some of these hesitant students may ask to speak with me privately. Once we are alone, the student will most often confide that he or she has always felt unloved and unlovable—as if they are a problem. They are always encouraged to know that I have felt the same pain and that I have been able to rise above it and make something of my life.

Just knowing that someone else understands seems to make it more manageable for them. I guess that is what it all really comes down to—not feeling alone with your pain. Knowing that they are not the problem but that they have a problem and, more importantly, understanding that they are not the only ones who have problems keeps them from feeling alone with their pain. This helps them to keep their hearts soft like the soil.

YOUR SUCCESS COVERS OTHERS ON RAINY DAYS

It had been eight years since I had seen my stepfather, Johnny Costen, pack his three boxes of belongings into the back of a cab. I had been told Johnny was excited about the scholarship that I had arranged for his son, John. I felt so good inside knowing that, in helping my little brother, I had also done something to help Johnny.

My brother was going to see Johnny that weekend that I was home for a visit. I decided to go with John to see my stepfather at my Aunt Shirley's home in Harlem. I knew Johnny would be both glad and surprised to see me.

The sky was a cloudy gray on the day my brother and I set out for my aunt's house. It had threatened to rain from the crack of dawn. The normal beehive of activity in the small project community of red brick buildings was devoid of traffic and was deathly still. Also missing was the usual chatter of housewives and retirees exchanging chit-chat across the courtyard from their living room windows.

We arrived at my aunt's house before Johnny and before the heaviest rain the city had experienced in years began to fall. I literally could not see the street from my aunt's kitchen window because of the volume of water that flowed over the panes of glass from the gutters above. As I considered the sheets of rain cascading in front of me, I tried to calm the strong feeling of excitement that filled my senses in anticipation of seeing Johnny. I worried about how he was traveling to Aunt Shirley's house. I hoped he had taken a cab instead of the train so he wouldn't have to walk from the train station up the two long New York City blocks.

I grew impatient as an hour passed without a word from Johnny. I asked my aunt to call him, but she didn't have a phone. I paced the floor like an expectant father or a college athlete waiting to see if he would be drafted into professional sports. More than once I wiped the condensation from the windows with a dish towel, trying to see if I could make out a human figure approaching the building, but it was impossible to see anything but the shadow cast by the oak trees outside Aunt Shirley's windows. As exasperation was about to overtake me, I heard the doorbell ring.

Johnny walked into the house soaked down to his bones. And while he did have an umbrella, it was clear that he had opted for the train because the lower portion of his pant legs was stuck to his skin. Small bubbles of moisture percolated through the ringlets in his shoes and out the sides between the stitching at the seams.

With obvious concern I asked, "Why didn't you take a cab?"

He replied in his typical Johnny Costen style, but with a frightfully unhealthy resonance to his voice, "I ain't goin' to waste my good money on no cab, when I can take the train. What? You think I'm stupid?" Then he flashed that broad, all consuming smile that made me feel so good inside. His voice, however, worried me.

He reached out for me and little John and gave us big hugs. It was the same hug that he had greeted me with when I was younger; a hug that I had longed for. We didn't say much for about five minutes. He had a lot to say to everyone but me. We just stared at each other, not in an uncomfortable way like people do when they are at a loss for words; instead the silence was reassuring. There were no ritualistic words for what we had to say to one another, but we were still communicating from our hearts.

He was studying me, taking in the measure of the manchild I had become. At eighteen, I stood 6'2" and weighed 200 pounds with almost zero body fat. I could see by the sparkle in his eye that he was proud of what I had become. I could sense that in the recesses of his mind for all of that reticent moment, he was congratulating himself for making a contribution to my success and at the same time regretting that he hadn't been party to the process.

I was basking in the chance to see Johnny. I studied his every move. I reacquainted myself with his mannerisms, his hairline, his mustache, the way he held his head to the side to make a point, and the quiet, gentle nature he possessed that he easily transferred to others. It just felt good to be around Johnny. Somehow I instinctively knew that there would be few people in my life that would make me feel this way, so I took in as much of this good person as I could. The sound of his voice scared me and I wondered if this would be the last time I saw Johnny alive.

It wasn't just his voice that gave me cause for concern, but also his attire which was terribly lacking. Absent was the silk laced 100% cotton French cuffed shirt, gabardine suit, winged tipped Stacey Adams shoes, cashmere overcoat and Fedora hat. They had been replaced along with the physical appearance of the man. I was saddened by the sight of the frail, swollen-faced man who represented Johnny Costen. His shirt was a bit soiled, frayed at the sleeves, and curled up at the collar's points. His shoes had rolled over onto their sides and were long past any semblance of respectability. The raincoat appeared to be borrowed, as it seemed a size too small, evidenced in the way the arm of his sports jacket protruded beyond the sleeve of the coat, a feature that in the past would have been below Johnny's standards of decorum.

I hurt for him all over again. I wanted to rescue him, but my blissful hope had passed and I conceded victory to the demon alcohol, the dream killer. I held back my urge to beseech him to give life one more try. Instead, I forced myself to just enjoy the moment with Johnny. Clearly his problem was having its way.

That day at my aunt's house evaporated like a desert spring when Johnny, Johnny Boy, and I reluctantly said our good-byes to Aunt Shirley. The storm had not let up when we headed out under the safe confines of Johnny's umbrella, into the mugging downpour. Johnny insisted that we take a cab. I tried to assume the protector's role and offered to walk him to the train station, but he would not have any of that option.

He hailed a cab for us with the wave of his arm. The gypsy cab skidded to a halt and Johnny grabbed the handle ushering us into its safety from the rain. Then he did something that would leave an indelible impression in my mind for the rest of my life. He marked my memory with the last image I would ever have of Johnny Costen.

With the grandest expression of parental devotion, he put forth a sacrifice to indicate his love for us and to perhaps symbolize a passing of the torch to me as his son's protector. He saw that I was what he had hoped that I would become under his tutelage. With chivalry, he reached into his pocket and pulled out a few dollars toward the payment of our fare and gave it to the cabbie, telling the driver our destination as if I at eighteen didn't know my address. But I understood the token of love for what it was, and held back my urge to interrupt him.

But then he caused my eyes to tear, and even now the tears well up and burst forward as I recall how he slowly folded up his tattered umbrella and passed it through the window to me. I said, "No Johnny, you keep it. You have to walk back to the train station. All we'll have to do is rush into the house from the cab."

But the torch had been passed, and he would not hear of taking it back. He demanded vehemently that I take it, that I allow him the privilege of giving. So, in spite of the anguish that I felt from leaving him unprotected in the rain, I understood the significance of his gesture and took the umbrella.

Then with a small tear in his eye he said he loved us and that he would see us soon. He told me to take care of myself and to look after my little brother. Most importantly, with inflection, he said, "I am so proud of you boys. And Robert, thank you so much for getting your brother into that good school."

And suddenly, the visit was over. The cabbie pulled the car away from the curb and once more pulled me away from Johnny Costen. My brother and I looked back through the window of the cab to see his small figure still standing there waving as the sheets of rain blanketed him, until finally the cab crossed over the McCombes Dam Bridge and sped us back into the Bronx.

My brother would see his dad on occasion during his visits home from the boarding school, but I never saw or talked to Johnny Costen again except to see his stone cold face sticking up from an inexpensive, brown casket. It was draped with an American flag in honor of the time he spent defending his country during the war. That flag seemed to return some sense of respect to this man who had lost it for himself.

But I never lost any respect for him. He was the only daddy I ever had, and God knows I miss Johnny Costen. I am sure that he is somewhere, watching me write this book along with my cloud of witnesses who are cheering me on to finish it.

Thank you, Johnny. And I'm still mad that you wouldn't let me beat you in a race to the porch, but I'm grateful you were there so I could try and so I could possess the knowledge of one of the greatest truths of all—that people are never the problem, they simply have problems.

LIVE IT!

CHAPTER 13

CHERISH THE GOOSE BUMPS

It is when people realize that they can never be a problem, that they really begin to live.

One day after exercising, I discovered a lump above my collarbone, and after an examination my doctor informed me that I had developed Hodgkin's disease—a very serious but highly treatable form of cancer of the immune system. You would think that I would have felt something when I received this information, but while my eyes watered, I did not cry. I was not able to feel the despair that such news normally brings.

I had long dreamed about becoming so sick or injured that people would have sympathy for me, pity me, maybe even love me. Perhaps the news would get back to my dad and he would come running to my side to support me through my last days. I had visualized the whole thing.

I didn't feel anything through the painful preparation for my cancer treatments nor the nauseating four months of chemotherapy injections, followed by five weeks of radiation and then another four months of injections. I had learned to deny myself the ability to feel.

In the beginning, not being able to feel enabled me to tolerate the reality of my situation and come to terms with the possibility that I might die. Instead of being concerned about the consequences, I simply went on with my life.

I was unable to cry about my condition, even when an allergic reaction to a medication left me with crippling hallucinations, insomnia, and thoughts of suicide. So severe were the symptoms that I considered jumping from my bedroom window. Fortunately, my wife was able to pull me away from the window and one of my brothers took me to the emergency room where a second drug was given to counter the effects of the first.

I felt the urge to cry. In fact, I never wanted to cry so much in my life, but I didn't know how. I felt inadequate. I wished for the feelings that cause goose bumps, even the ones that signal that you are scared to death. But I could not summon one single feeling. My mind was numb; I was just existing, taking up space.

SURVIVORS HELP OTHERS SUCCEED

During my orientation at the Stanford Medical Center, a social worker invited me to participate in the

Cancer Survivors group she facilitated at the hospital. But I resisted subjecting myself to the possibility of facing my feelings about my cancer. The idea of admitting that I was sick was the last thing I wanted to think about. I had learned to deal with things by exerting my will against them or by redefining the situation.

I did get through the treatment, but not without a price. I refused to acknowledge the fear and vulnerability I had experienced in my brush with death. Over the next six years, I romanticized the illness. I talked about it as if it were a scene in a movie. However, even in my fantasy as an actor I didn't do what was fundamental to acting. I did not assume the feelings and attitude of the character. The reality was that I couldn't feel anything about what I had been through.

But God is merciful. At the age of forty-one, after six years of pain and suffering accompanied by a deep depression, I agreed to talk with Pat Fobair, the survivors group facilitator from Stanford. In one hour with Pat, I was able to gain more clarity about my inability to feel than I had from the four psychiatrists with whom I had previously consulted.

Pat taught me that feelings originate in thought, and thought comes from experiencing things that occur in your surrounding environment. Then she provided me with an illustrated model that I could take home. The model served as a focus point when I had feelings of intense anxiety and depression. Pat approached me like an intelligent human being who had a problem. She talked to me and provided materials that allowed me to help myself.

But the primary thing that turned my situation around was what I learned while sitting in the survivors group. One night, a young Latin woman entered the group. She had recently completed her therapy for lymphoma, and cried every time she attempted to talk about her pain. Finally she was able to put together a few sentences. She spoke about not being able to feel good about anything, and about her feeling unlovable. She said that she was unable to enjoy the things in life that used to give her joy, like going to the movies or taking long walks with her boyfriend.

She told the group that she was deeply depressed and anxious about dying. She expressed confusion over the fact that she had not felt those feelings when she first learned of her illness or even during the time she was undergoing the sickening and painful chemotherapy treatments.

PEOPLE WITH PROBLEMS AREN'T ALONE

For the first time, I heard someone else talking about what I had experienced, and suddenly I realized that I was not the problem but that I had a problem. When I shared with her that I had been experiencing the same thing, we immediately felt relief in our identification with one another. A sense of hope came over us. She began to cry tears of joy, but I could produce nothing but a broad smile.

Within seconds another group member said some magical words to me. She said, "Robert, last week you talked about a feeling of depression that descends on you whenever you have a joyful thought."

"Yes!" I replied.

"I spent many years in a depressed condition myself. My depression was triggered by troubling thoughts rather than joyous ones, but I believe what I discovered during that time might help you better understand your own situation."

I leaned forward, determined not to miss one word of what she was about to say. "The human brain has a tremendous capacity to translate what we experience into thought, which gets turned into feelings. Both the good and the bad of our experience gets processed in this fashion. What the brain cannot do is pick and choose. If the brain decides not to feel pain, it also loses the ability to feel pleasure. In order for the brain to experience feelings of pleasure it must leave its emotional door open to feelings in general allowing both pain and pleasure to have access to the human being."

To Feel Joy You Must also be Willing to Feel Pain

I hadn't realized that to feel joy I must also be willing to feel pain. Suddenly I saw my situation with a greater clarity than I have ever known. For the next few weeks, I practiced consciously allowing myself to accept a pleasurable experience for what it was, rather than avoiding it. I attempted to do the same when a painful situation presented itself. Slowly but surely, I began to feel less anxiety in situations that in the past would have made me feel uncomfortable.

One day the survivors group was involved in a discussion about how stress can make us vulnerable to cancer. I was sharing my story about how my dad had not returned for me and Pat was acknowledging my strength and courage for enduring my setback and turning a negative into a positive. Suddenly, my chest began to tighten, my pulse began to race, and I felt tingling all over my face and up and down my arms and legs. The symptoms were familiar because they had occurred several times before. To me, they seemed to be signaling a heart attack.

Pat (a survivor herself) and the rest of the group reassured me that I had nothing to worry about. They too had experienced similar symptoms. I learned that what I was experiencing was my inability to accept Pat's compliment. By accepting it as truth, I would have to allow myself to feel the pleasure associated with it.

Throughout the week I held onto that thought, and whenever I felt those sensations I conditioned myself not to panic. Slowly the sense of panic dissipated.

Now when I experience something painful, I accept it for what it is, a portion of the "feelings mosaic," which also includes that which is pleasurable. Why was I now able to get in touch with my feelings? Because for the first time, I was beginning to understand that I was not a problem—I only had problems.

SUCCESS IS FEELING PASSIONATE TOWARDS LIFE

Knowing that I was not the problem allowed me to come a little closer each day to appreciating the full value of my existence on this planet and learning to celebrate the wonderful contributions God has allowed me to make. I knew my healing was progressing, when finally, one day, after turning forty-one, I felt a special warmth overtake me as my eleven and nine-year-old sons embraced me with a huge hug and a kiss right in front of their schoolmates. Even though the kids jeered them a bit, they never relaxed their hold on me.

As the three of us walked across the campus together, my six-year-old daughter spotted us and took off running in my direction yelling "Daddy!" as loud as she could. She was celebrating my arrival. With her arms spread wide and her eyes lit up like a 1,000-watt Christmas light, she jumped into my arms and gave me a big hug.

In that moment, with all three of my children surrounding me with their love, I felt an outbreak of goose bumps all over my body, and for the first time in a long while, I wanted to live!

It is as children that we first freely allow ourselves to feel the full gamut of emotion. We enjoyed goose bumps then; now as adults we must learn to cherish them.

To be like a child means to be free to feel great disappointment, yet accept great happiness moments later. Anyone who has been around children has seen their amazing ability to start laughing in the midst of rolling tears. Children embrace the unexpected joy that causes goose bumps.

As we humble ourselves to be like children again, we will expect the best in everyone we meet, just as children do. What changes would come into our relationships if we could adopt the theory that others are innocent until proven guilty? Perhaps our communication towards others would be more graceful if we understood that people are never the problem, but people have problems.

To be like a child means to trust others with open interest. Children have to be taught to retreat from strangers, but adults must learn to recognize those who may need the human exchange of respect and encouragement. When you demonstrate love to people who have problems, you position yourself to enjoy the greatest blessings of your life.

MAYBE THEY WERE ANGELS

You are God's primary resource in the earth to help others rise above their problems.

"Keep on loving each other as brothers. Do not forget to entertain strangers, for by so doing some people have entertained angels without knowing it."

Hebrews 13:1,3 NIV

I believe with all my heart that God has been directing my efforts as I have written this book. I also believe that He has placed many inspiring people in my life to whom I am grateful for their values and whose character records are beyond reproach. They are not perfect, but they are the type of people who are soft enough to admit their mistakes and ask for forgiveness. They look for ways to make things right, and refuse to turn their backs on strangers, or the poor, or the homeless, or those afflicted in their bodies and spirits.

These people taught me to keep believing, to never give up on others, to always see the good in people, and to find the courage and the faith to love others even when they don't appear lovable. These are the people who taught me that I was not a problem.

I trust that I have learned their lessons well. I have prayed for righteous muscles so that I could push my ego aside and accept others for who they are rather than what I want them to be.

I have come to understand that the times when I am most successful at loving people are the times when I am mirroring the attitudes these special people have about life. From them I have learned that we are responsible for our fellow human beings. To wit, that we are each our brother's keeper and God has no other earthly means that He uses to bring us His messages of love.

We should be motivated to be kind to one another, and to look after each other as brothers and sisters. We should treat others with hospitality and consider this great possibility: maybe they are angels!

I hope this book has been spiritual nourishment to your soul and helped you to understand that *people are never the problem; people simply have problems.*

I challenge you to live what you have resolved in your heart to do while reading this book.

Strengthen yourself to be a problem solver.

Optimize your abilities to build up others.

Acknowledge those who have helped you.

Rejoice when you see others succeed.

Once you have learned these keys to success, teach others the four steps to **SOAR**ing on their own. Explain to them that they will get where they want to go by helping others get what they need. Encourage them to:

Strengthen others,

Optimize their admirable attributes,

Acknowledge them and

Rejoice when they help others succeed, too!

You will **SOAR** to new heights with a crowd of witnesses cheering for you as you help others to also succeed in life. You are God's primary resource in the earth to help others rise above their problems. I pray that you will learn to embrace this truth, because the world needs you on God's team.

MY TRIBUTE TO THOSE WHO HELPED ME SOAR

My Tribute To Those Who Helped Me SOAR To Success, And Who Have Taught Me To Treat People Like Angels

Mr. Michael Choukas
My Headmaster at Vermont Academy—Mr. Choukas taught me humility.
Mrs. Anita Choukas
My drama teacher at Vermont Academy
Bob and Marti Harrington
My dorm parents at Vermont Academy—Mr. Harrington taught me patience.
Mr. Dwight Jones
My one and only roommate at Vermont Academy—DJ-True-blue to the end
Mr. Ernie Castagner
My basketball coach at Vermont Academy—A man of great passion
Mrs. Hellen Frey
The infirmary nurse at Vermont Academy—My mother away from home
Mr. Jack Peters
My English teacher at Vermont Academy—The man who inspired me to write my first poem and gave me peace of mind
Mr. Stephen Hardy
My Latin teacher at Vermont Academy —He taught me confidence.
The Brocato Family
Milford, Massachusetts.
Bobbie Gene and Phyllis Stewart Family
Reading, Massachusetts—The salt of the earth
Mr. Greg Stewart
Danvers, Massachusetts—My brother from day one, a gentle soul
Mrs. Millie Butler
Bronx, New York —My second mother
Mike and Debbie Ledford
Tucson, Arizona—The holders of pure love
Mr. Roger Garcia
New Mexico—A friend forever
George and Veronica Smith
Kentfield, California.—Beholders of the faith
Chuck and Michelle Butler
Walden, New York
Chuck
The brother my mother couldn't birth

The Butler Family
Bronx, New York

Luther Jones
Milan, Italy—The brother my mother couldn't birth

Luther and Joan Jones
Bronx, New York—They always made their hearts available to me.

Mr. Timothy Edmondson
Oakland, California

Mr. Samuel Norman
Oakland, California—The mentor, and a man who is not afraid to cry

Mr. Sylvester Jackson
My late friend who helped me to keep my sanity after my forced retirement from football

Byron and Sparti Hemingway
Seattle, Washington—My brother in Christ

Mr. Johnson
Bronx, New York—The first man who took the time to drive my friends and me to our ball games

Leon and Barbara Stamps
Boston, Massachusetts

Leon
The brother my mother couldn't birth

Mr. Thomas Frye
San Francisco, California

Mr. Thurman V. White
Newark, California

Mr. Lawrence MacFaden
My cousin and the person who inspired me the most to be someone, even when my professional football career was cut short

Mrs. Dorothy Morton
My Mother—Thank you Lord for her.

Mr. Charles Morton
My late stepfather

Mr. and Mrs. Chip Wolcott
The Orme School—Mayer, Arizona

Mrs. Grete Sorensen
My mother-in-law and the person in my life who always tries to understand

Mr. Eric Sorensen
My late father-in-law

Mr. Joseph Yukica
My football coach at Boston College—Thank you for letting me be myself, Coach.

Mrs. Greenspan

My eighth grade teacher at PS 73 in the Bronx—She really loved me and convinced me that I was lovable. God bless you and keep you wherever you are.

Mr. Westler

My gym teacher at PS 73 in the Bronx

Mr. Townsend

My seventh grade teacher at PS 73 in the Bronx

Ms. Turner

My sixth grade teacher at PS 11 in the Bronx

Mr. and Mrs. Quinn

My Aunt and Uncle in Harlem, New York—They always made time to care.

Mrs. Lillian Irving

Queens, New York—My Auntie and her friend Wally, who are bearers of unconditional love

Mr. Jim Schoel

My second mentor when I was fifteen and the person that helped me to get into prep school.

Mr. Billy Thomas

My first mentor and the person that made sure I got onto the right path at the age of twelve.

Mr. London

My late friend and the first man I ever loved like a father.

Mrs. Francis Hunt-Stewart

Pacifica, California—A friend for all seasons.

Mr. John H. Costen

My late stepfather and the man who taught me to walk and helped me to make my first snowball.

My Cancer Survivor Group at Stanford Medical.

Robert and Michelle Gossett

Los Angeles, California

Dr. Kenneth Blanchard

Rancho Bernardo, California—A man of peace, with a warm and strong belief in all humankind

Dr. Rudolph E. Busby

My graduate advisor at San Francisco State University and the person whose confidence, patience, and excellent mentoring I used to buoy me during my three years of masters work in speech and communication studies

Mrs. Sharon Robinson

San Leandro, California

Scott & Cecilia Jones

Concord, California

Ms. Nancy Mims
Oakland, California
Senator Bill Bradley
Who during a summer basketball camp in Harlem, New York told me that being successful in sports would mean nothing if I did not get an education
Mr. Gordon Moody
Vermont—A man of compassion and vision
Neal Green
Middlebrook, New York
Larry Medcalf
San Francisco, California—My graduate adviser and the person who admitted me to graduate school at San Fancisco State University
Aliza & Kinney Christian
Richmond, California
James and Helen Nassikas
Mill Valley, California—Two people who I love dearly
Mr. Nassikas
A premiere hotelier and a leader who stewarded his employees with the greatest humility
Joe Reilly
Ross, California
Mr. Brodine
Saxtons River, Vermont
Lloyd Lawrence
Oakland, California—A man of honor
Angie Rios
Fresno, California
Rick Williams and Ingrid Merriwether
San Leandro, California—My dearest friends
Dennis Jeffrey
Oakland, California—A bearer of the cross
Lloyd Lawrence
Oakland, California—A man of honor
Peter Dwares
San Francisco, California—A man who trancends race
Keith Barnett
Newton, Massachusetts
Neil Green
Middlebrook, New York

Phillip Hazzard
Providence, Rhode Island

And To Those Virtuous People Who Hold Me Together:
My Brothers:
James Connor—A man of PERSEVERANCE
Willie Young—A man of COURAGE
John Costen—A man of LOVE
My Sisters:
Connie Jean Connor—A woman of GRACE
Andrea Blischke
Iris Blischke
My late sister:
Francis Ann Connor—She was her brothers' keeper
who brought me to Christ. I will always love you, Sis.
My wife:
Ellen Watts—A ROCK
My Children:
Robert Watts III—A boy with a VISION
Jeremiah Eric Watts—A loving boy
Erika Robyn Watts—She makes dreams come true.
My Nieces and Nephews:
d'Artagnan Conner
d'Artagnae Ariel Connor
d'Arquoia Frances Connor
Elizabeth Coney
Rhonda Conner
Lori Toney
Dorothy Connor
James H. Connor III
Tesha Connor
Anette Connor
John C. Costen
Alonda Greer Young
Carmel Young
Bricesha Young
My Father, Robert Watts Sr.
A man who finally faced his problems

BIBLIOGRAPHY

Anson, Robert S. *Best Intentions: The Education And Killing Of Edmund Perry.* New York: Vintage Books, 1987.

Applebaum, Ronald L. , et al. *Fundamental Concepts in Human Communication.* San Francisco: Garfield Press, 1973.

Bales, Robert F. *Interaction Process Analysis.* Cambridge: Addison-Wesley Press, 1951.

Bales, Robert F. *Personality and Interpersonal Behavior.* New York: Holt, Rhinehart and Winston, 1970.

Bales, Robert F. *Symlog: A System for the Multiple Level Observation of Groups.* New York: The Free Press, 1979.

Blanchard, Kenneth and Michael O'Connor. *Managing by Values.* San Francisco: Barrett-Koehler Publishers, 1997.

Blanchard, Kenneth. *We Are the Beloved: A Spiritual Journey.* Grand Rapids: Zondervan Publishing House, 1994.

Burke, Kenneth. *Language as Symbolic Action: Essay On Life, Literature, and Method.* Berkeley: University of California Press, 1966.

Busby, Rudolph E. and Randall E. Majors. *Basic Speech Communication: Principles and Practices.* New York: Harper & Row, 1987.

Davis, Bruce and Genny Davis. *The Magical Child Within You.* Fairfax: Inner Light Books and Tapes,1982.

Folger, Joseph P., et al. *Working Through Conflict: A Communication Perspective.* Glenview, Ill.: Scott Foresman. 1984.

Gibb, Jack. "Defensive Communication." *Journal of Communication.* 1961.

Hansberry, Lorraine. *"A Raisin In The Sun."* Random House, 1959.

Heider, Fritz. *The Psychology of Interpersonal Relations.* New York: John Wiley and Sons, 1958.

Lewin, Kurt. *Principles of Topological Psychology.* New York: McGraw-Hill, 1936.

Luft, Joseph. *Of Human Interaction.* Palo Alto: National Press Books, 1969.

Miller, William A. *The Joy of Feeling Good: Eight Keys to a Happy & Abundant Life.* Minneapolis: Augsburg Publishing House, 1986.

Mitchell, Grace. *A Very Practical Guide To Discipline With Young Children.* Telshare Publishing, 1982.

Simonton-Matthews, Stephanie, O. Carl Simonton, M.D., and James L. Creighton. *Getting Well Again.* New York: Bantam Books, 1984.

Spitzberg, Brian H. "Communication Competence As Knowledge, Skill, and Impression." *Communication Education.* (July 1982).

The American Medical Association: *Family Medical Guide.* New York: Random House,1987.

The Random House College Dictionary. The Unabridged Edition. New York: Random House, 1982.

Webster's New World Dictionary: Third College Edition of American English. New York: Prentice Hall, 1994.

About the Author

Robert Watts Jr. was born and raised in the Bronx, New York. He attended public school in New York City and at the age of fifteen accepted a special grant to attend Vermont Academy (VA) in Saxton River, Vermont. While at VA he excelled in sports, earning All-Prep honors in track and field, football, and basketball. In his senior year he captained both the football and basket-  ball teams to undefeated seasons. He was also recipient of the coveted Voice Literary Award for poetry.

In 1973, Robert entered Boston college on a football scholarship. As a freshman and sophomore, he played tight-end for the Eagles. In his junior year, he switched to linebacker where he made the All-Eastern College Team and All-American his senior year.

In 1977, he was drafted by the New Orleans Saints in the third round of the NFL draft. Spinal injuries cut his career short, but not before he had a chance to play for the Oakland Raiders in 1978.

In 1983, he was inducted into the Vermont Academy Sports Hall of Fame. With his football career over at the age of twenty-six, Robert entered graduate school at San Francisco State University and in 1986 he graduated with a Master's Degree in Speech and Communication Studies.

In 1997, he was inducted into Boston College Varsity Club Hall of Fame. He was also named an honorary member of the Vermont Academy Board of Trustees.

For inquiries write to:

Robert Watts Jr.
New Dawn Productions
1320 North Van Ness Avenue
Fresno, California 93728

Additional copies of this book
are available from your local
bookstore.

Honor Books
Tulsa, Oklahoma